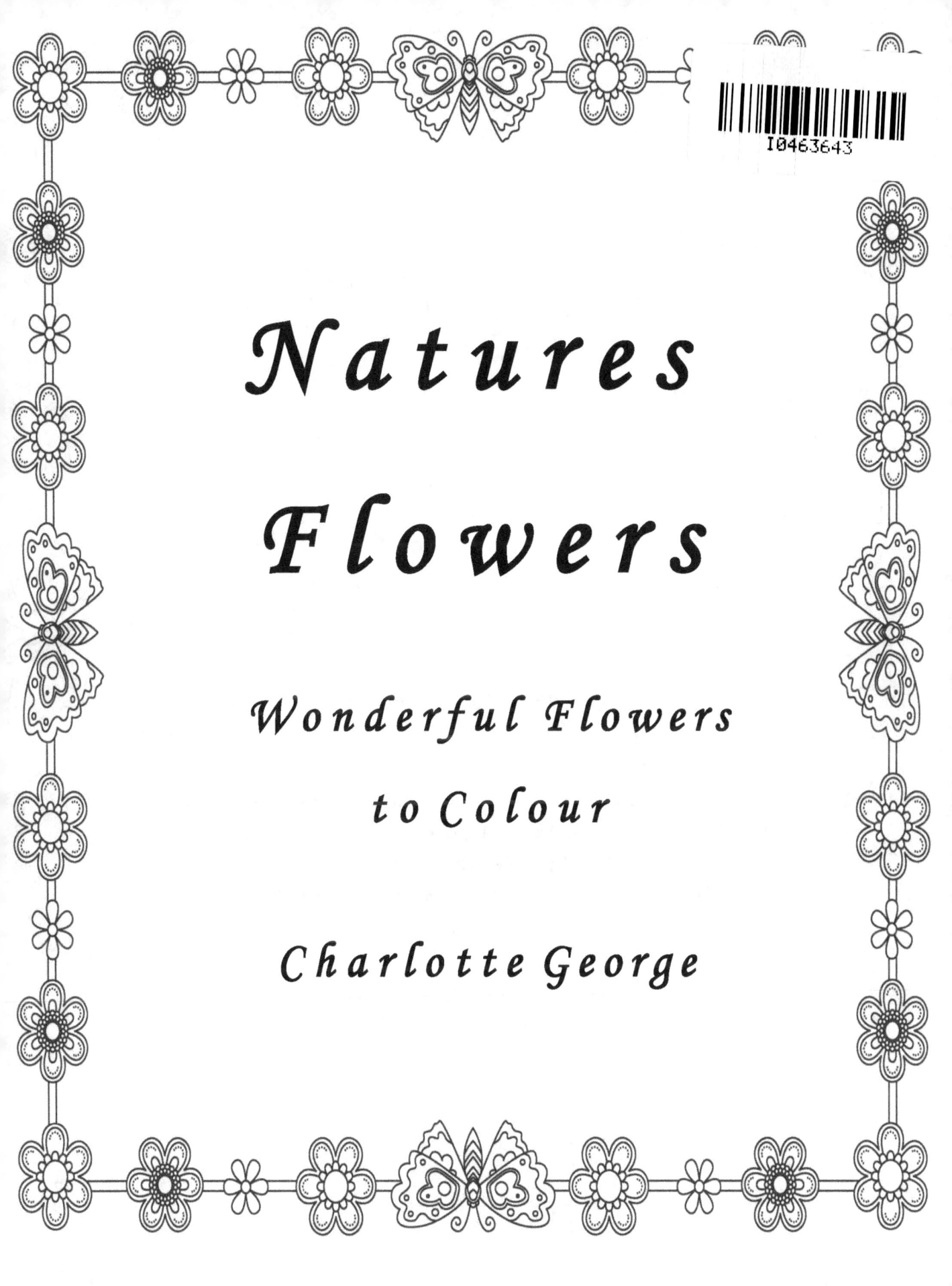

Natures Flowers

Wonderful Flowers to Colour

Charlotte George

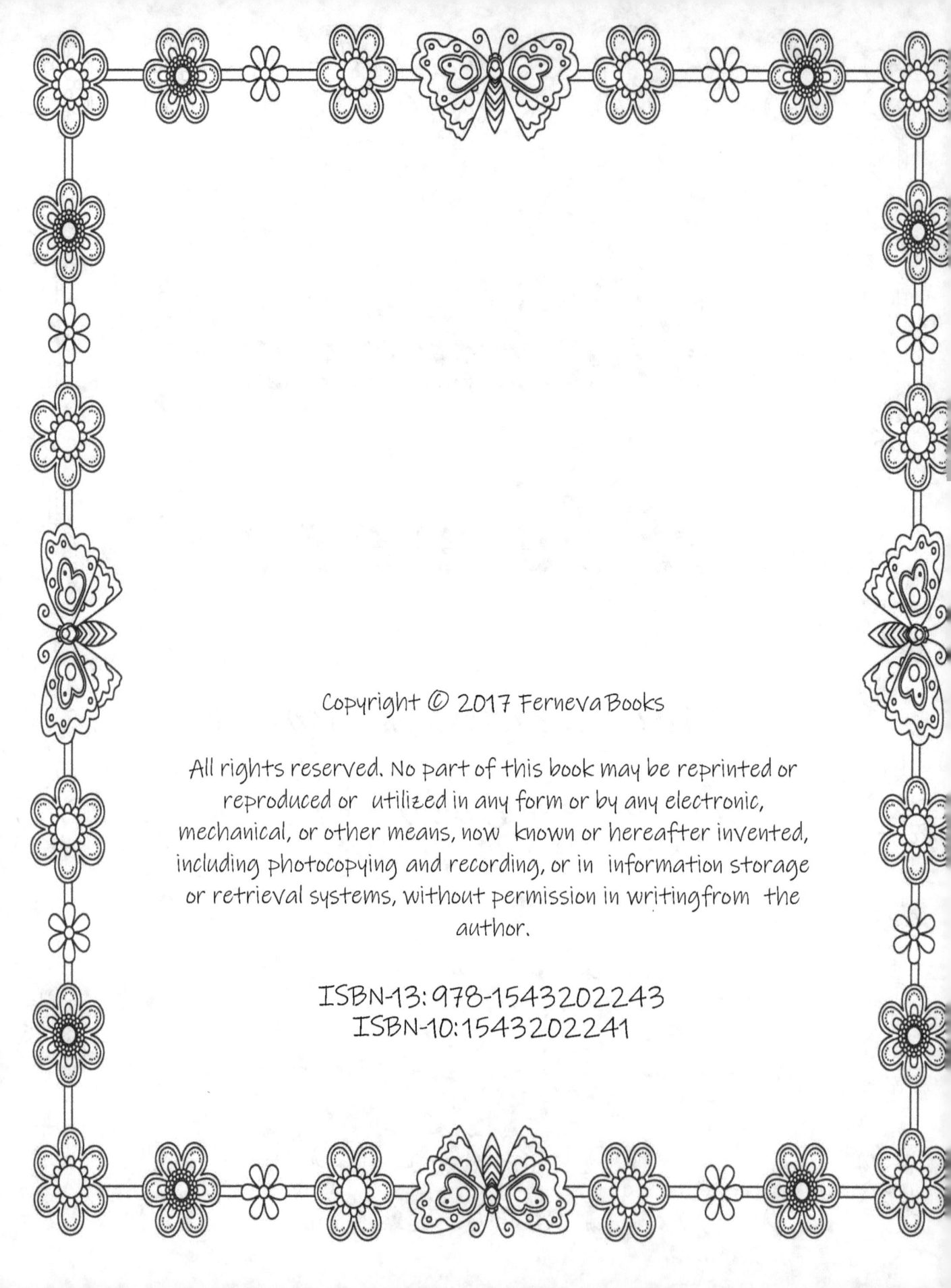

ISBN-13: 978-1543202243
ISBN-10: 1543202241

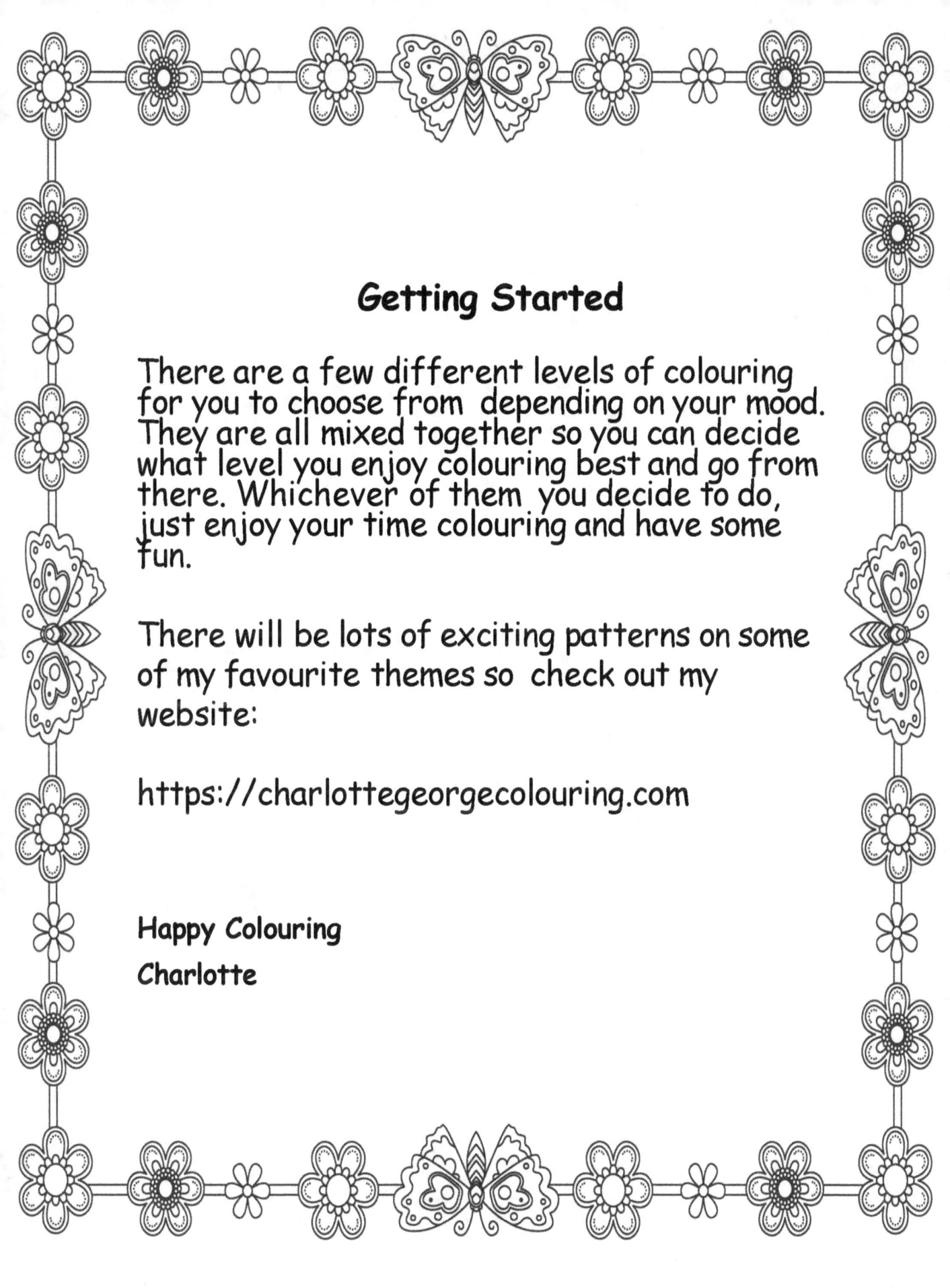

Getting Started

There are a few different levels of colouring for you to choose from depending on your mood. They are all mixed together so you can decide what level you enjoy colouring best and go from there. Whichever of them you decide to do, just enjoy your time colouring and have some fun.

There will be lots of exciting patterns on some of my favourite themes so check out my website:

https://charlottegeorgecolouring.com

Happy Colouring

Charlotte

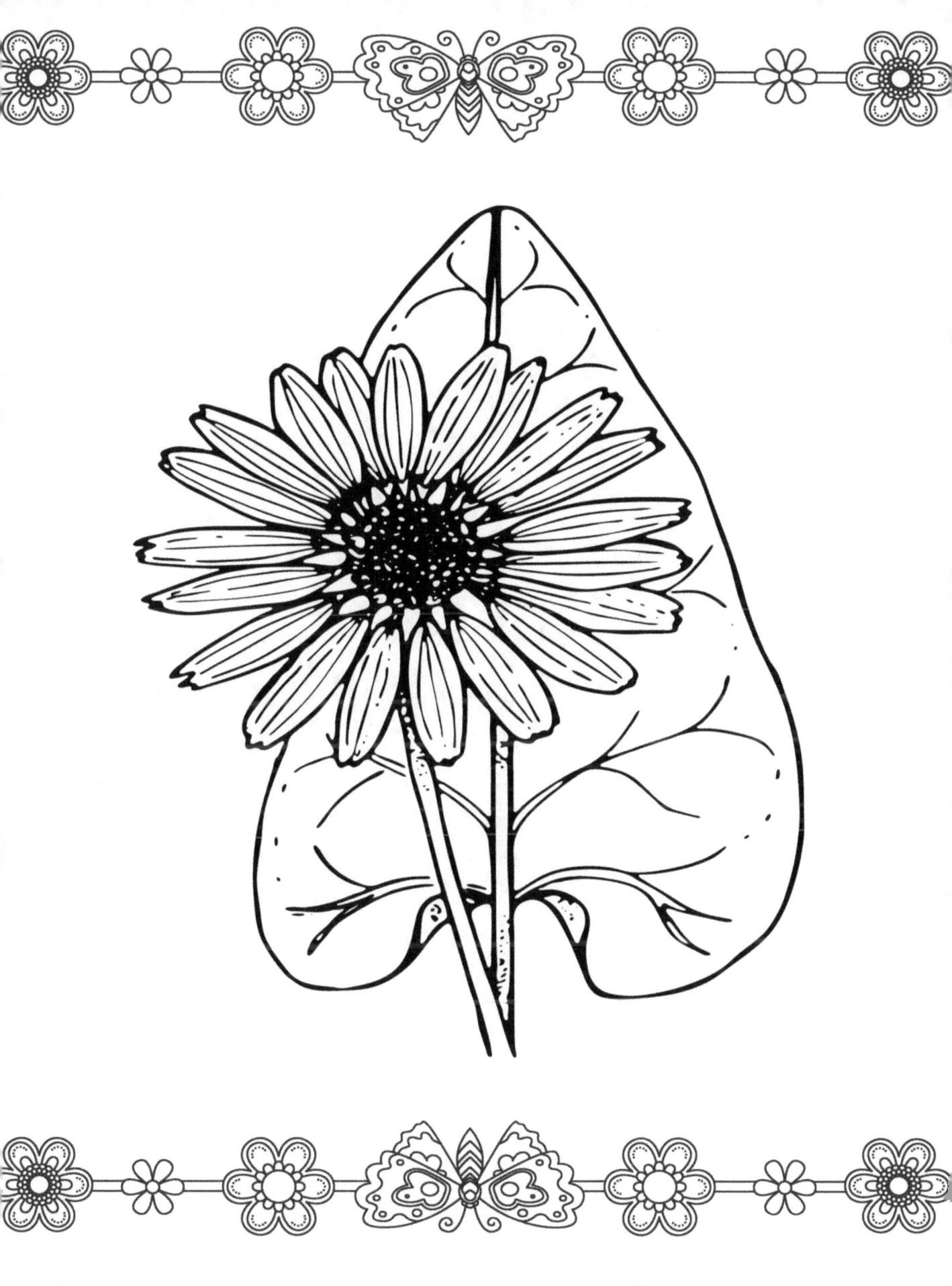

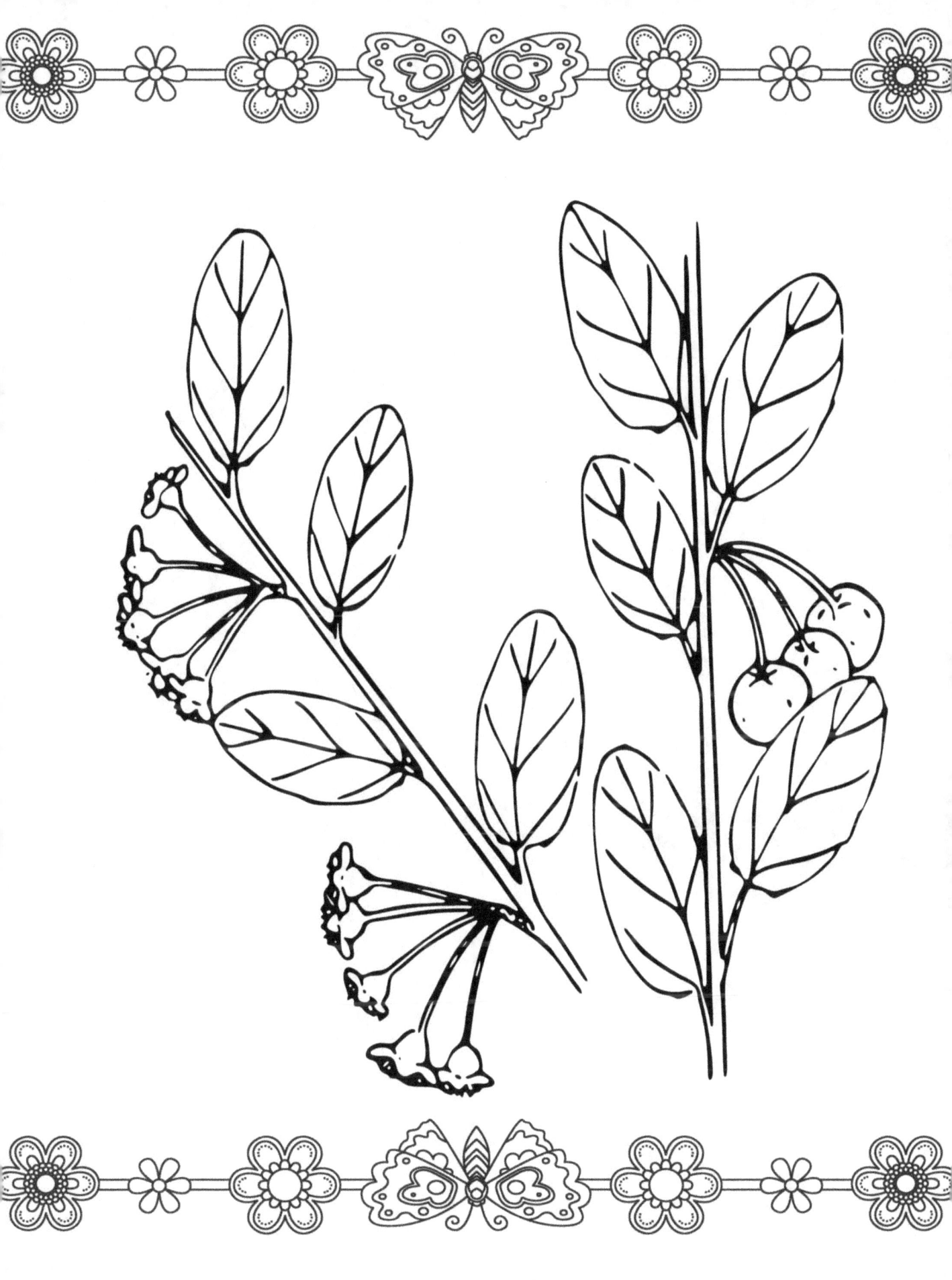

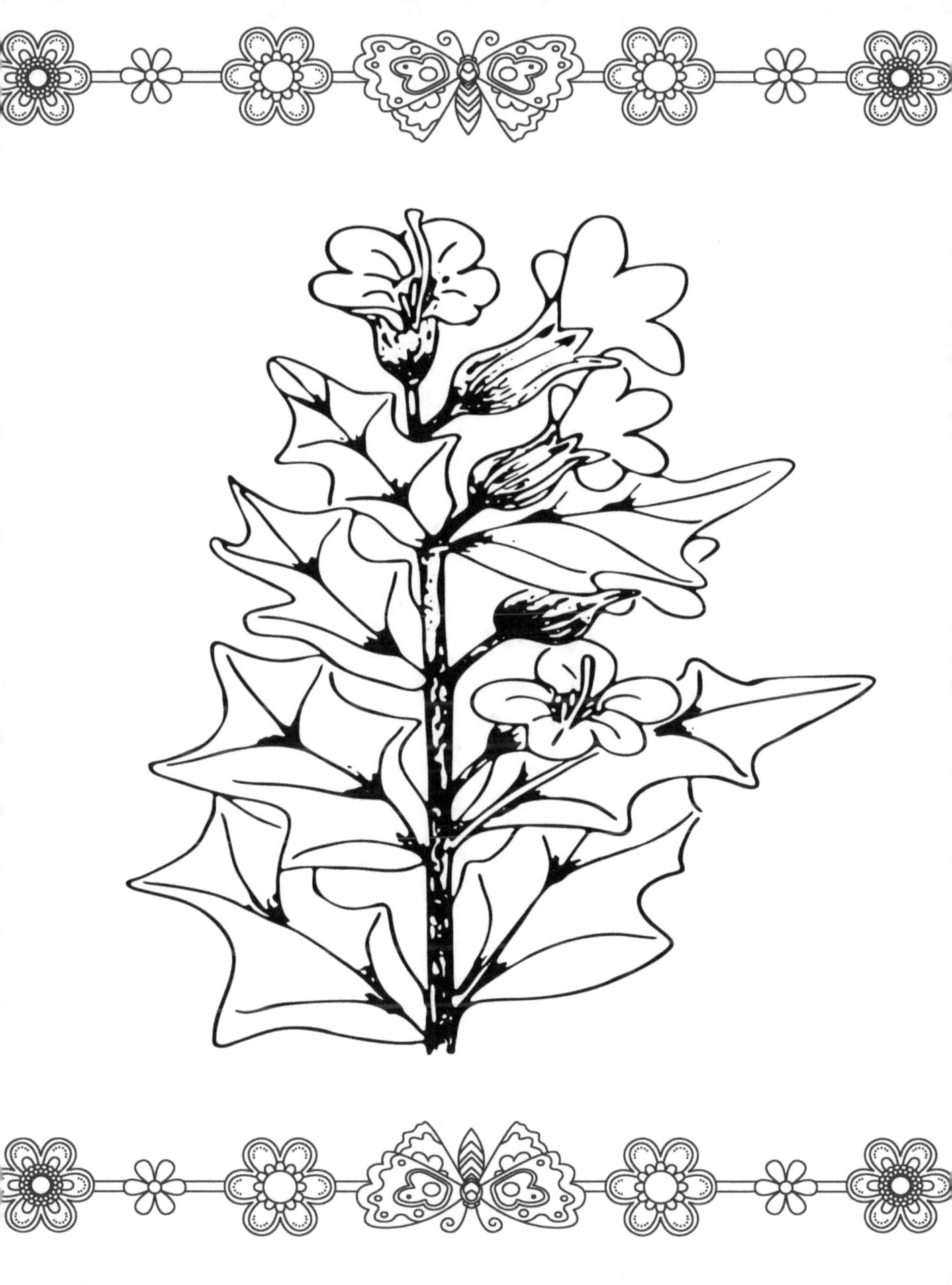

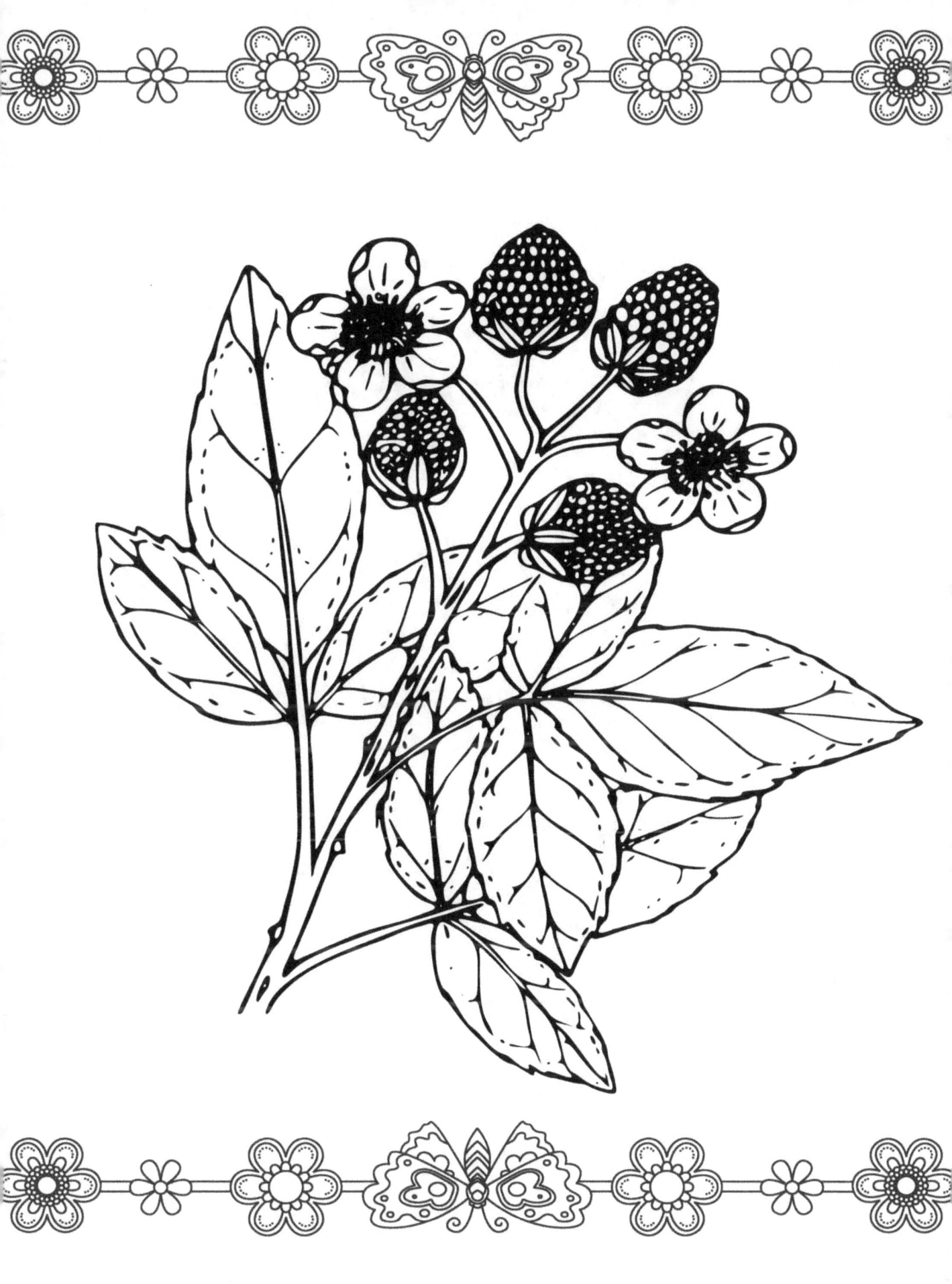

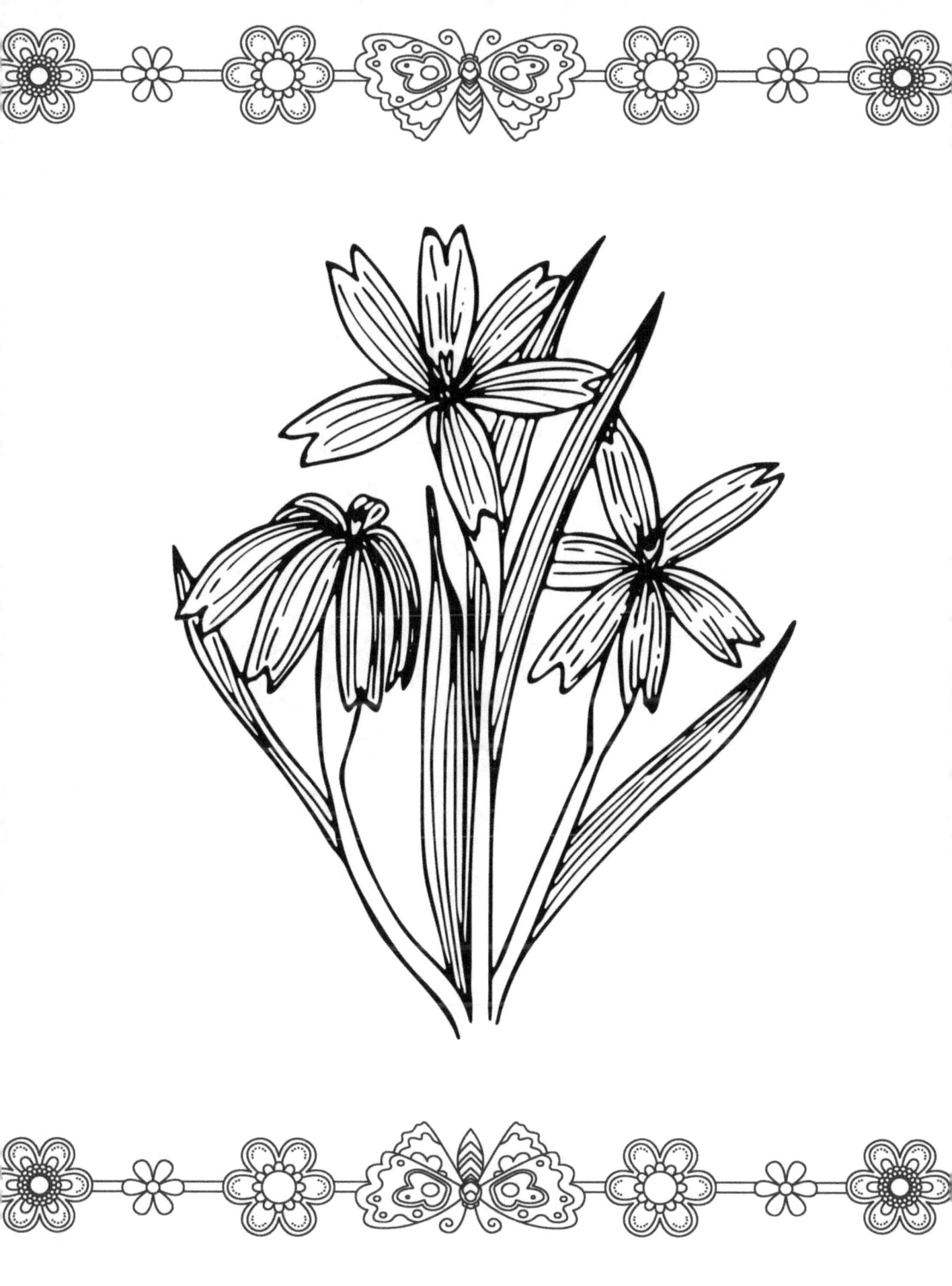

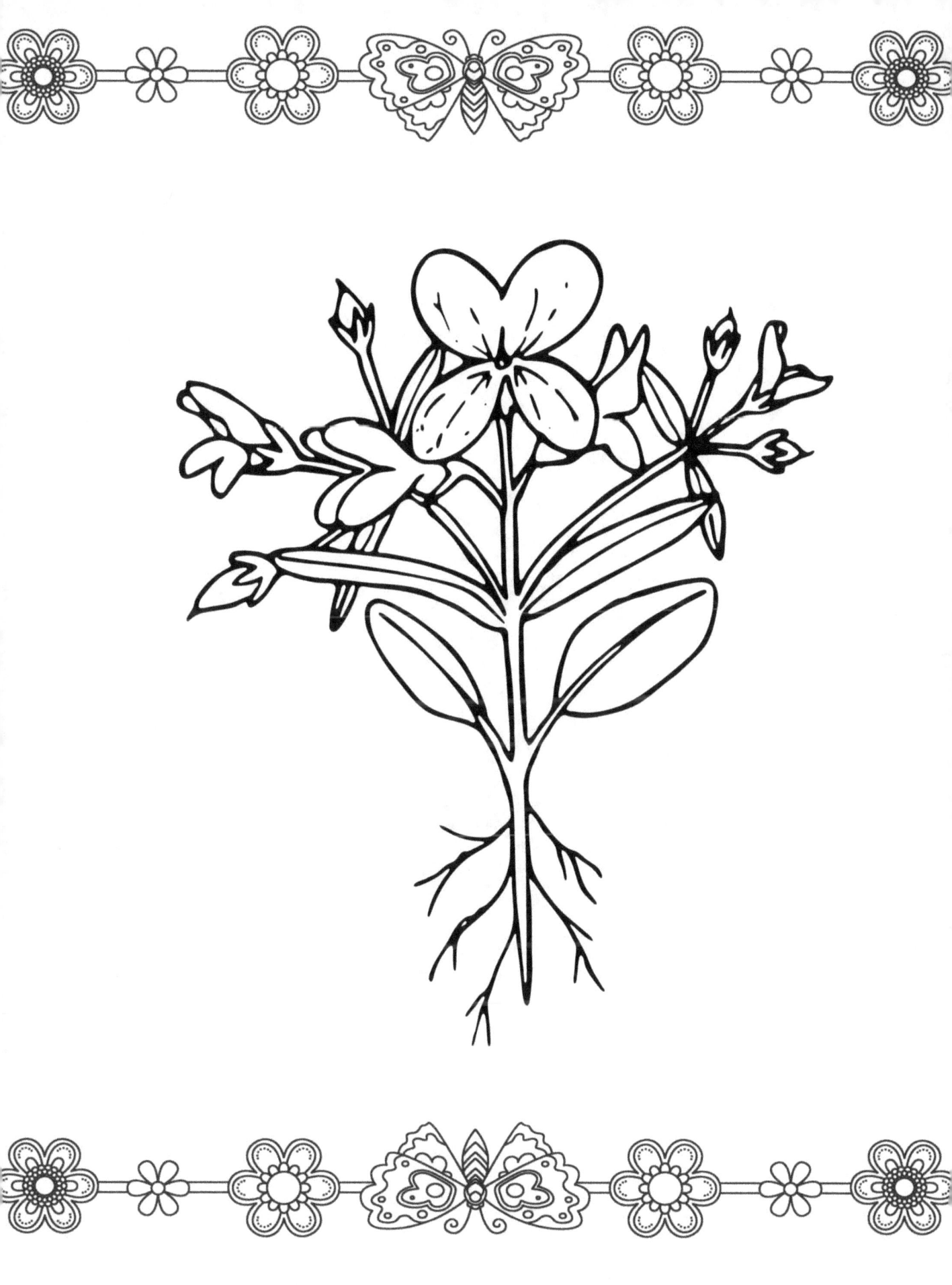

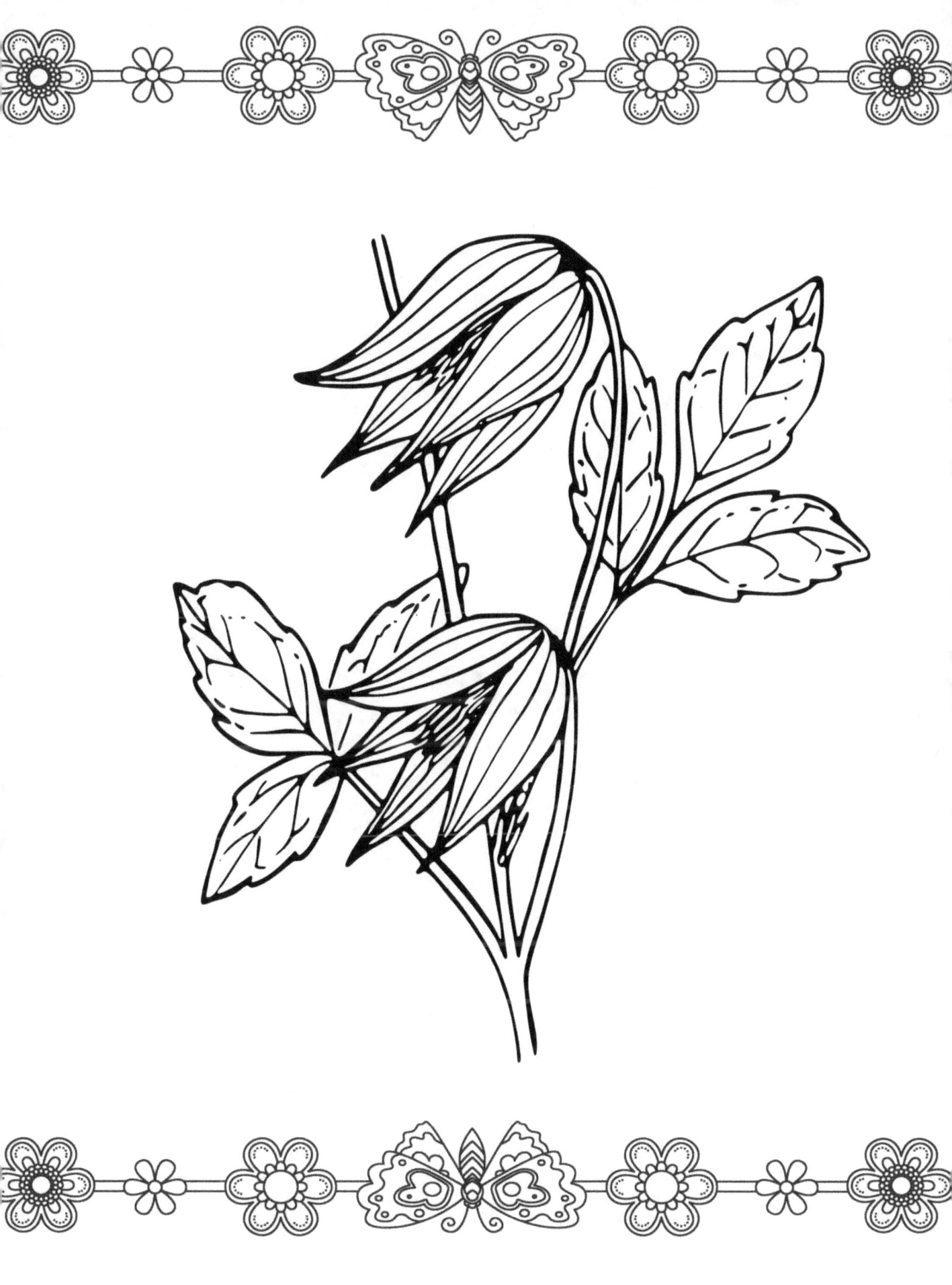

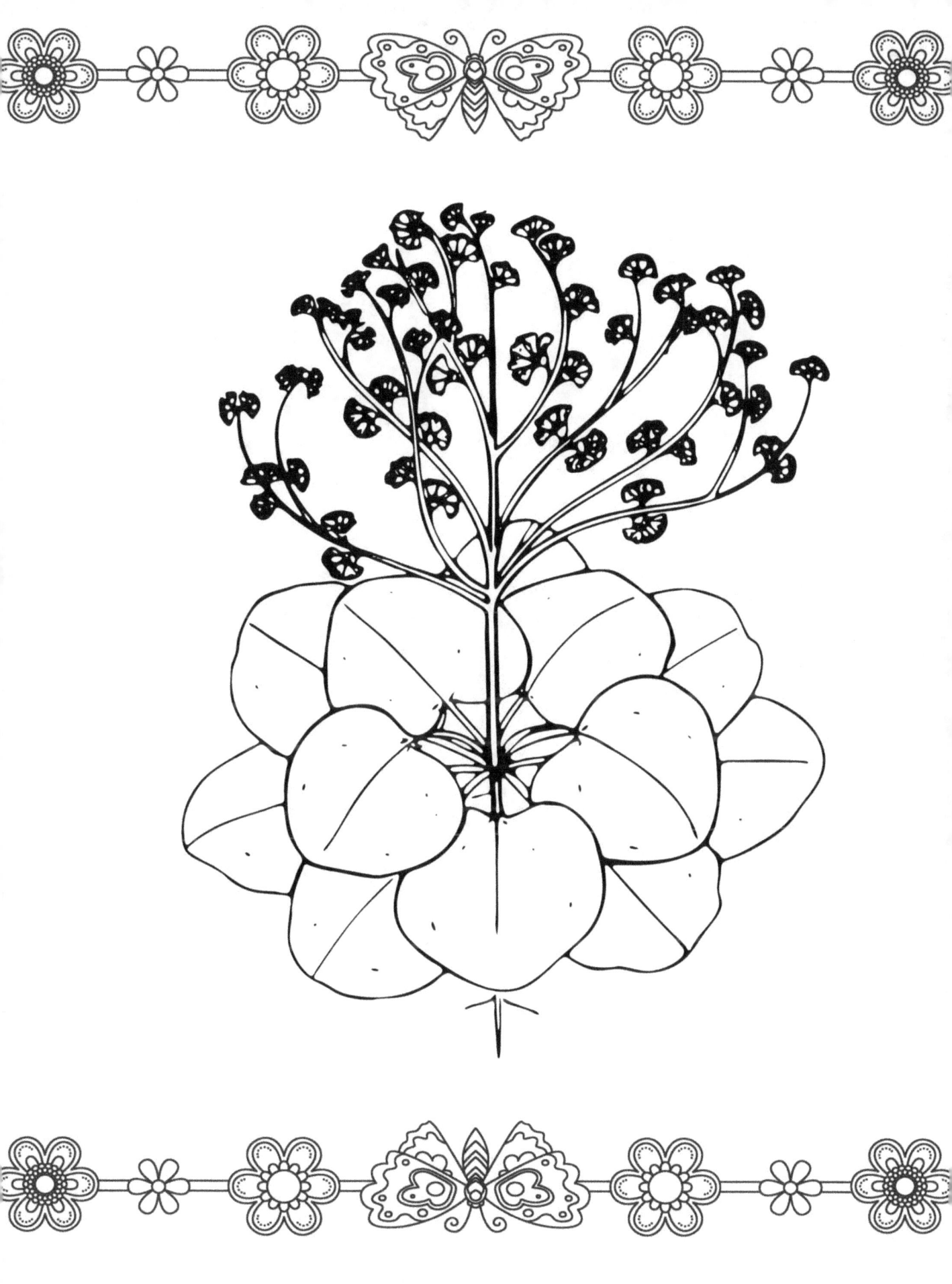

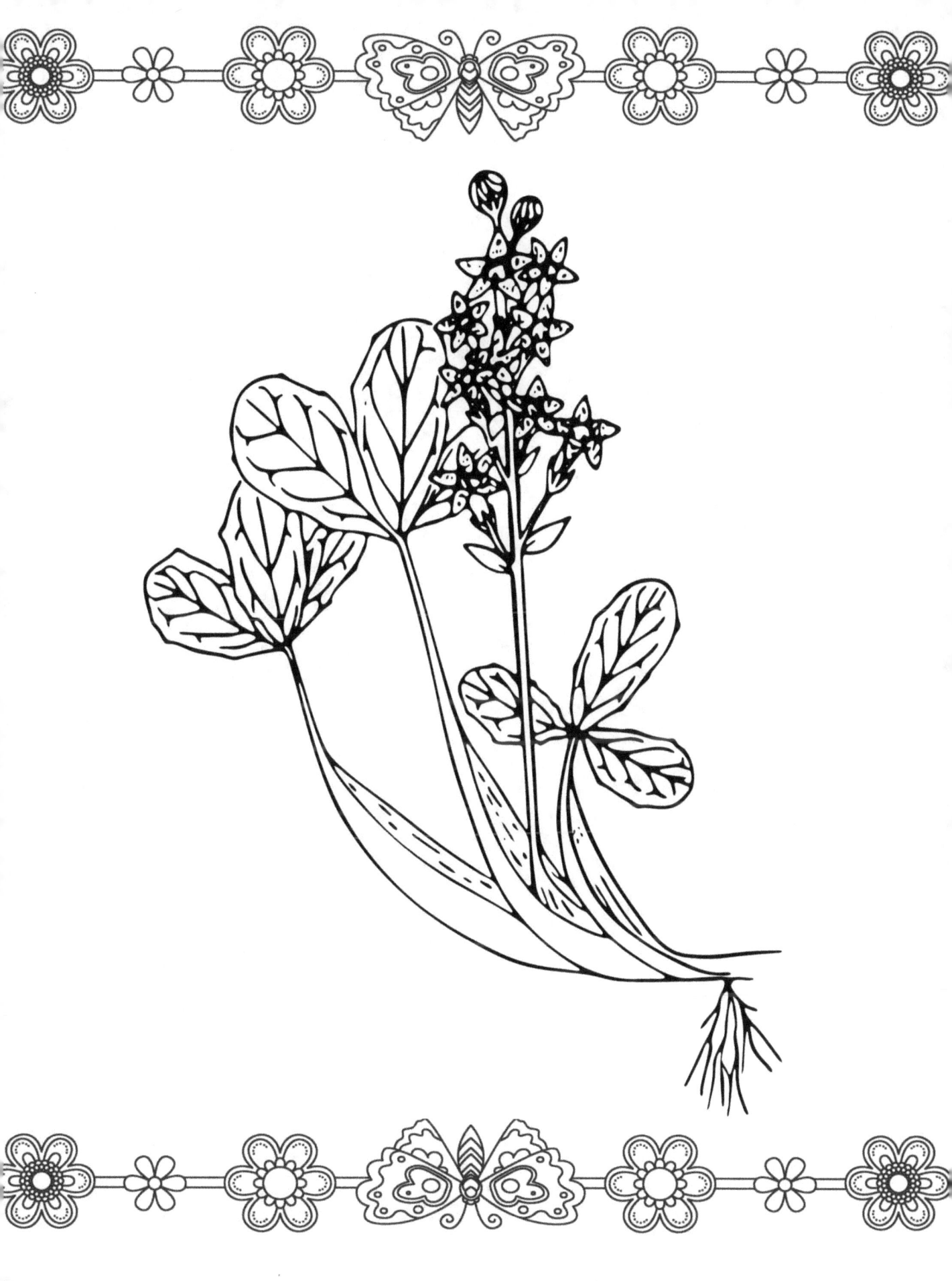

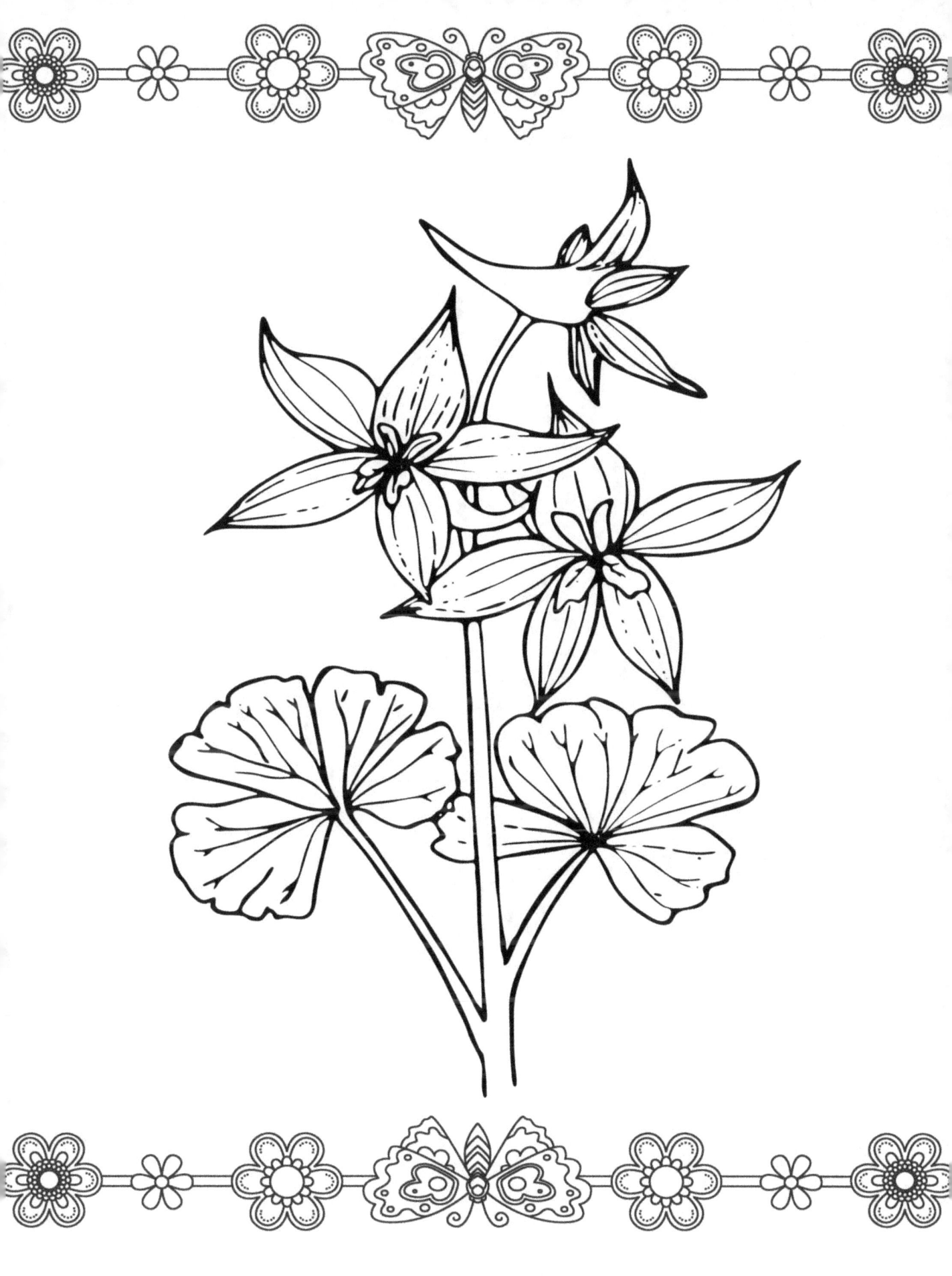

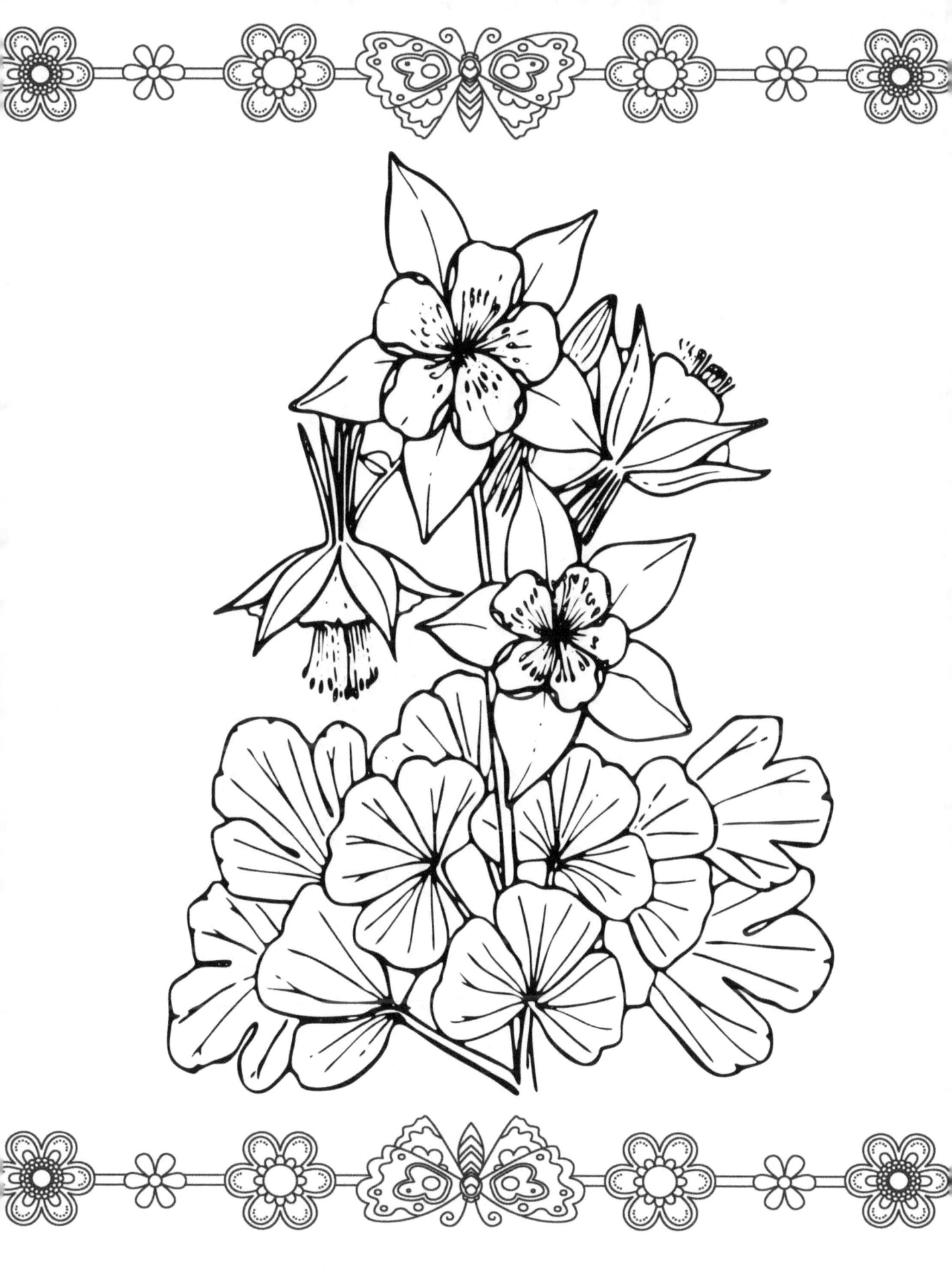

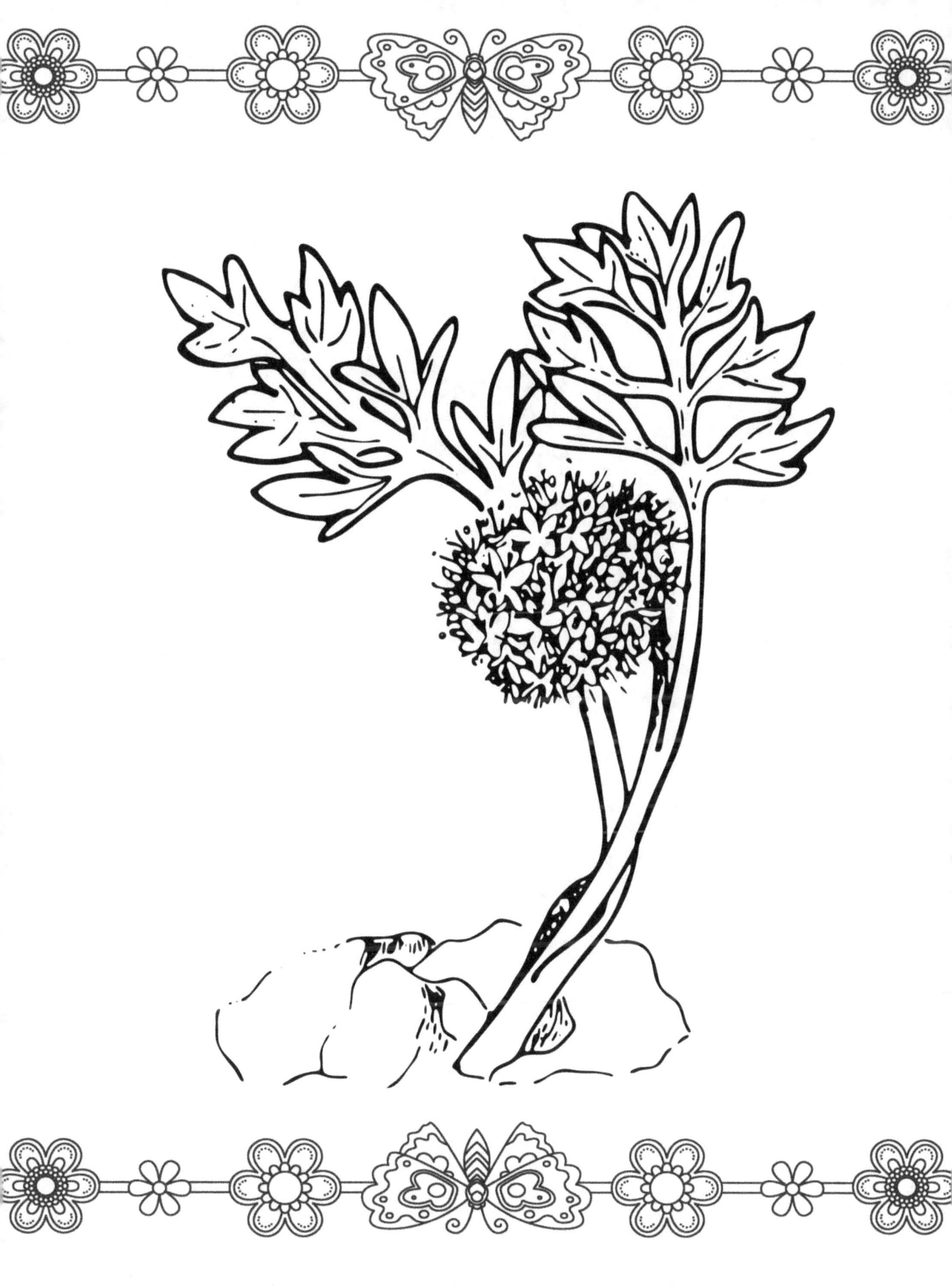

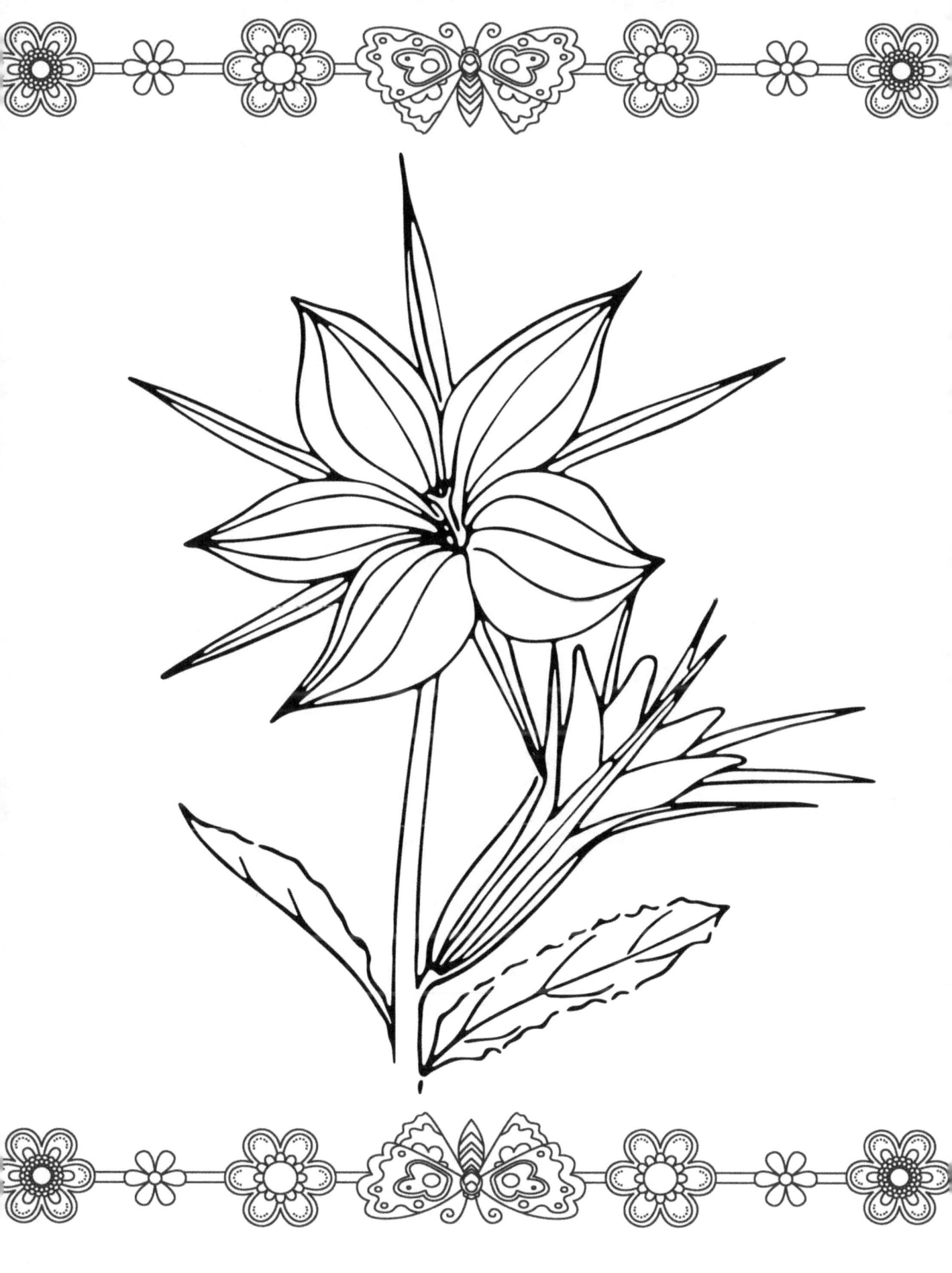

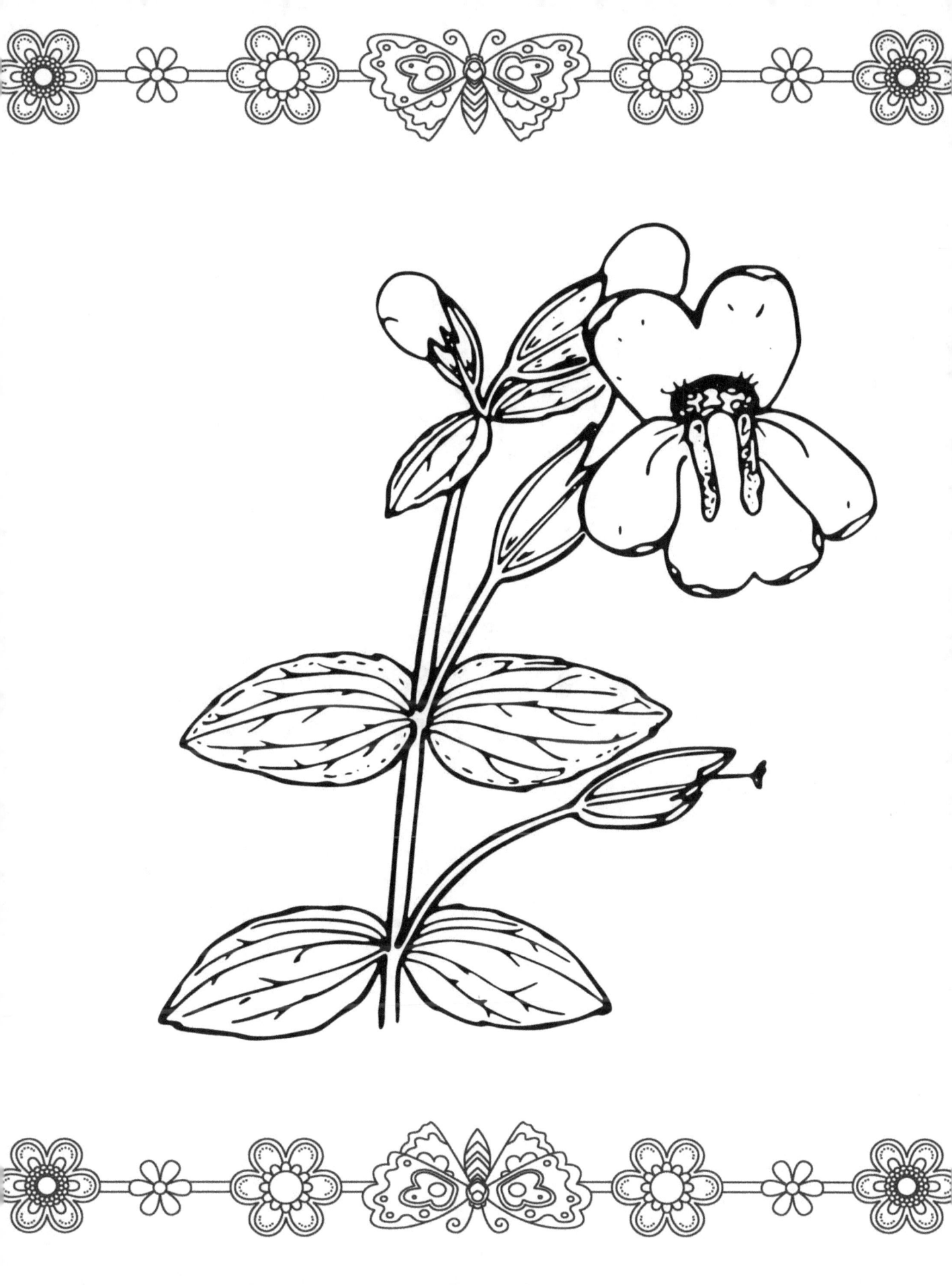

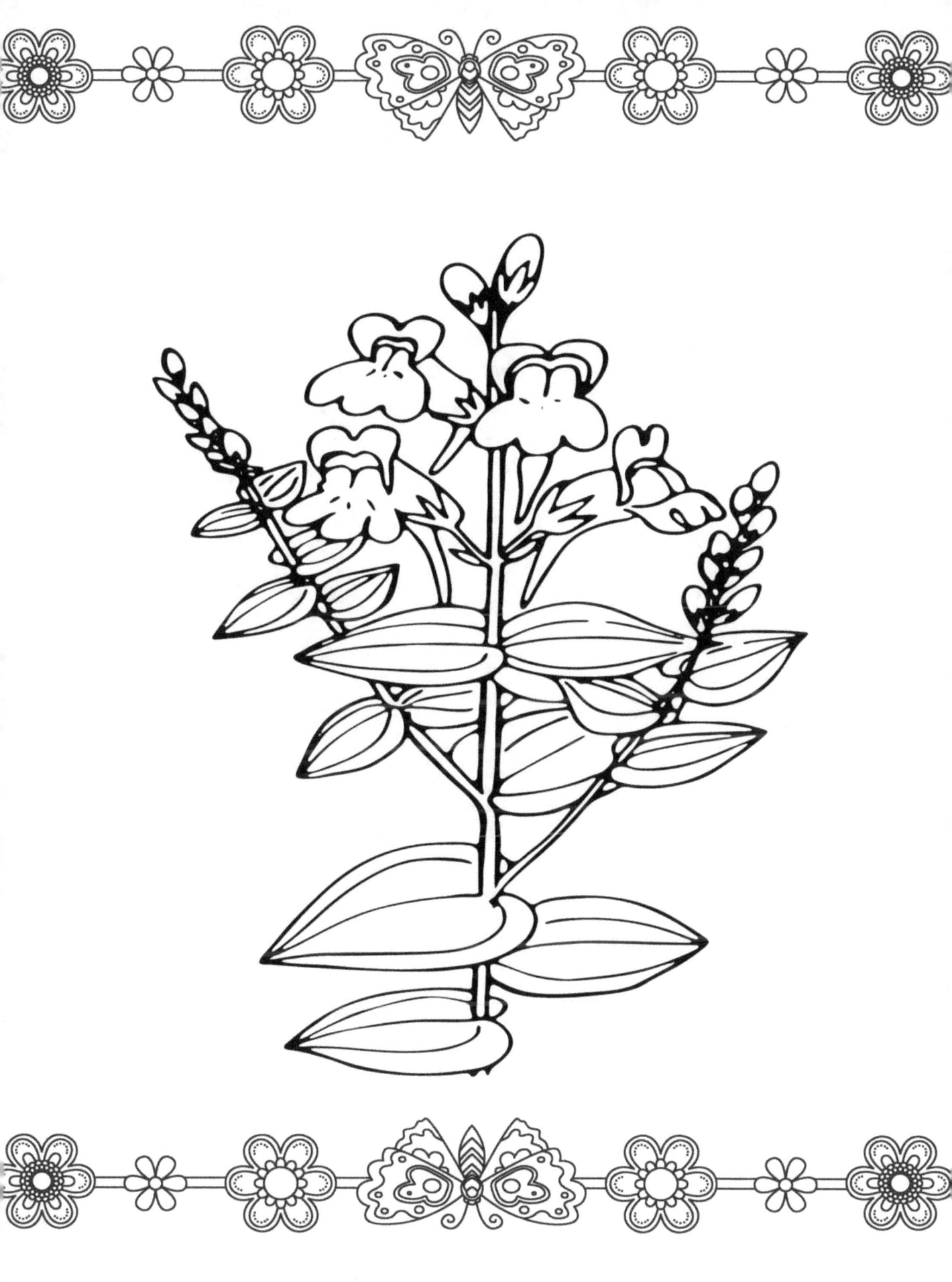

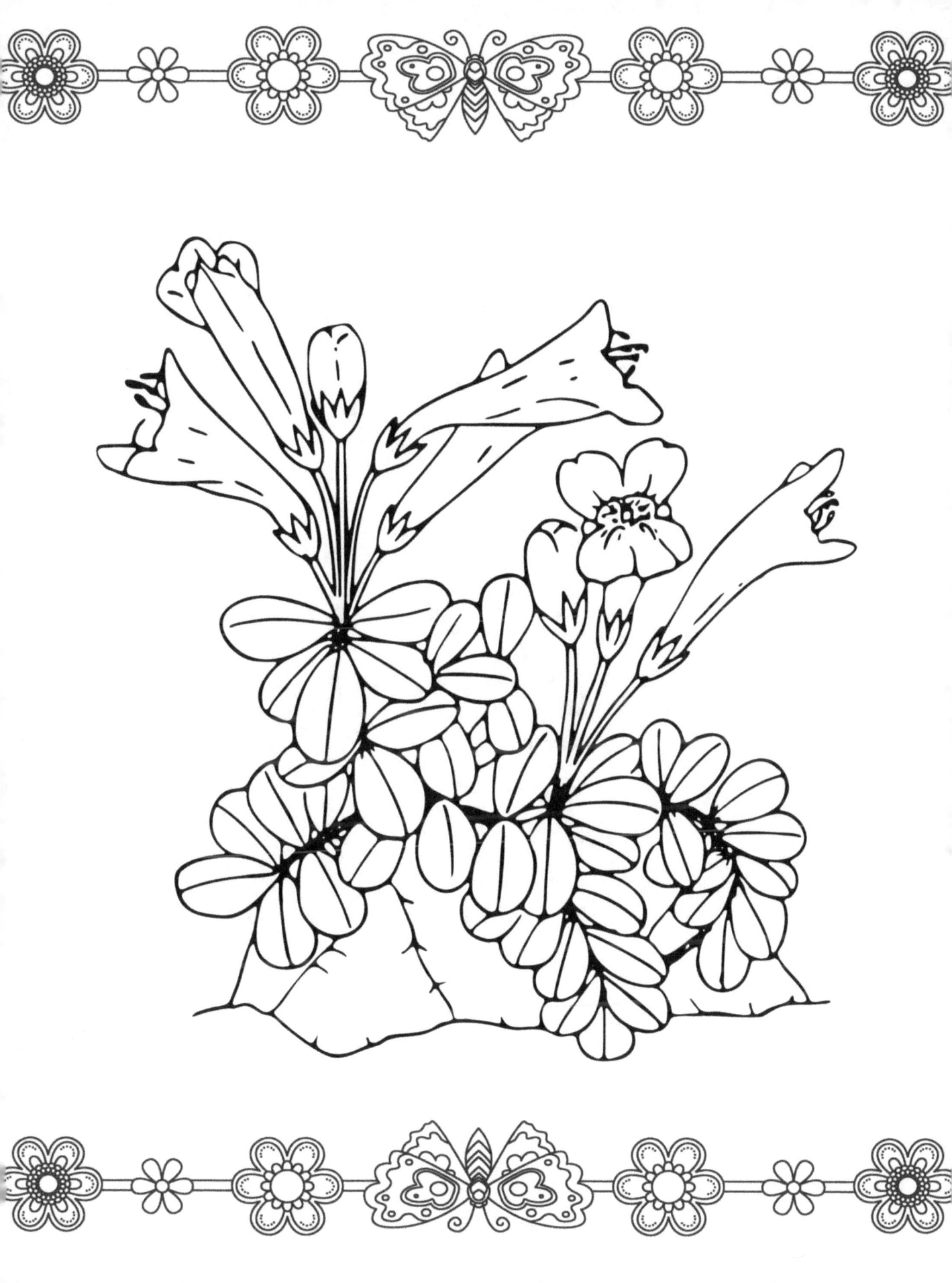

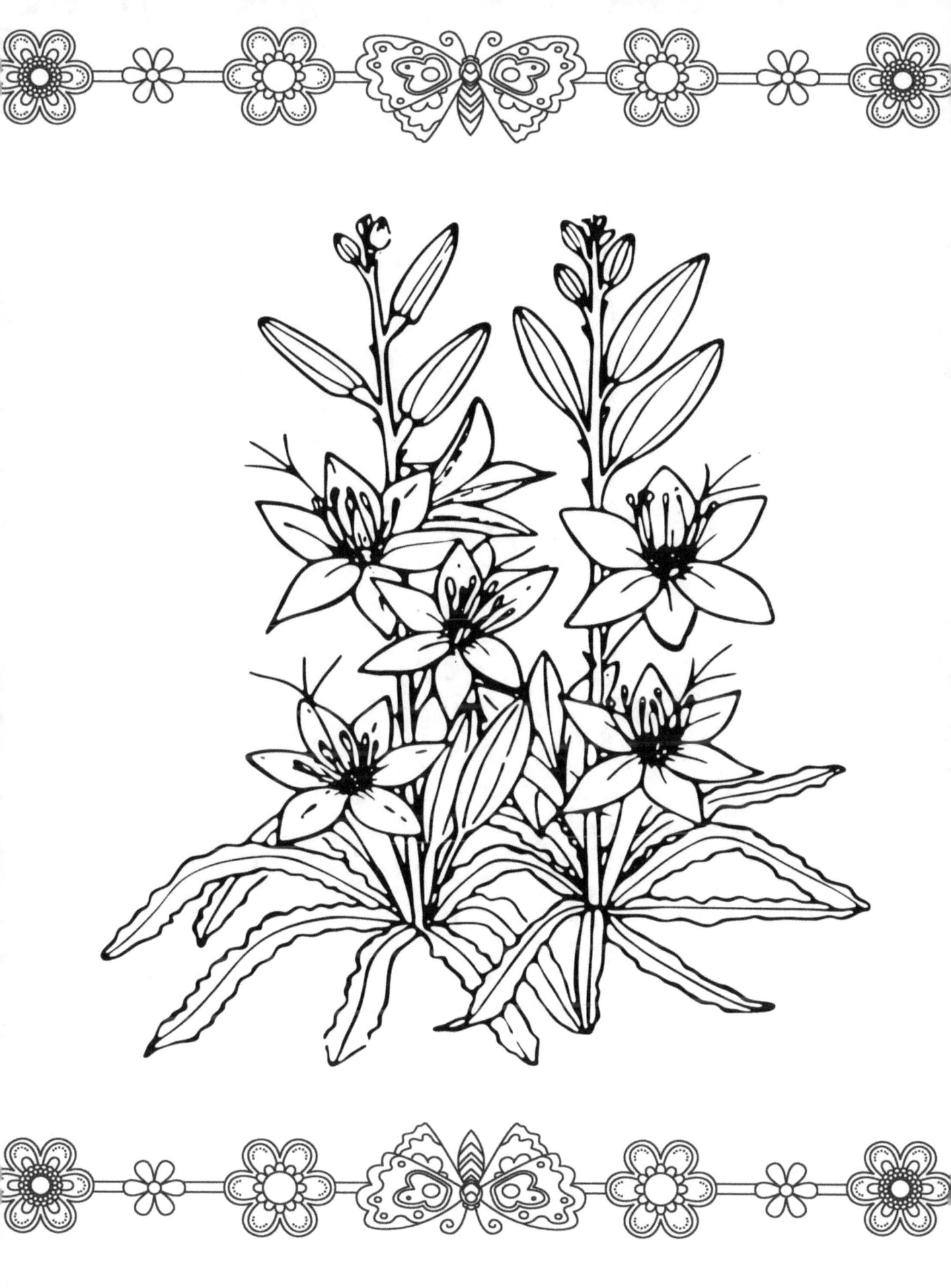

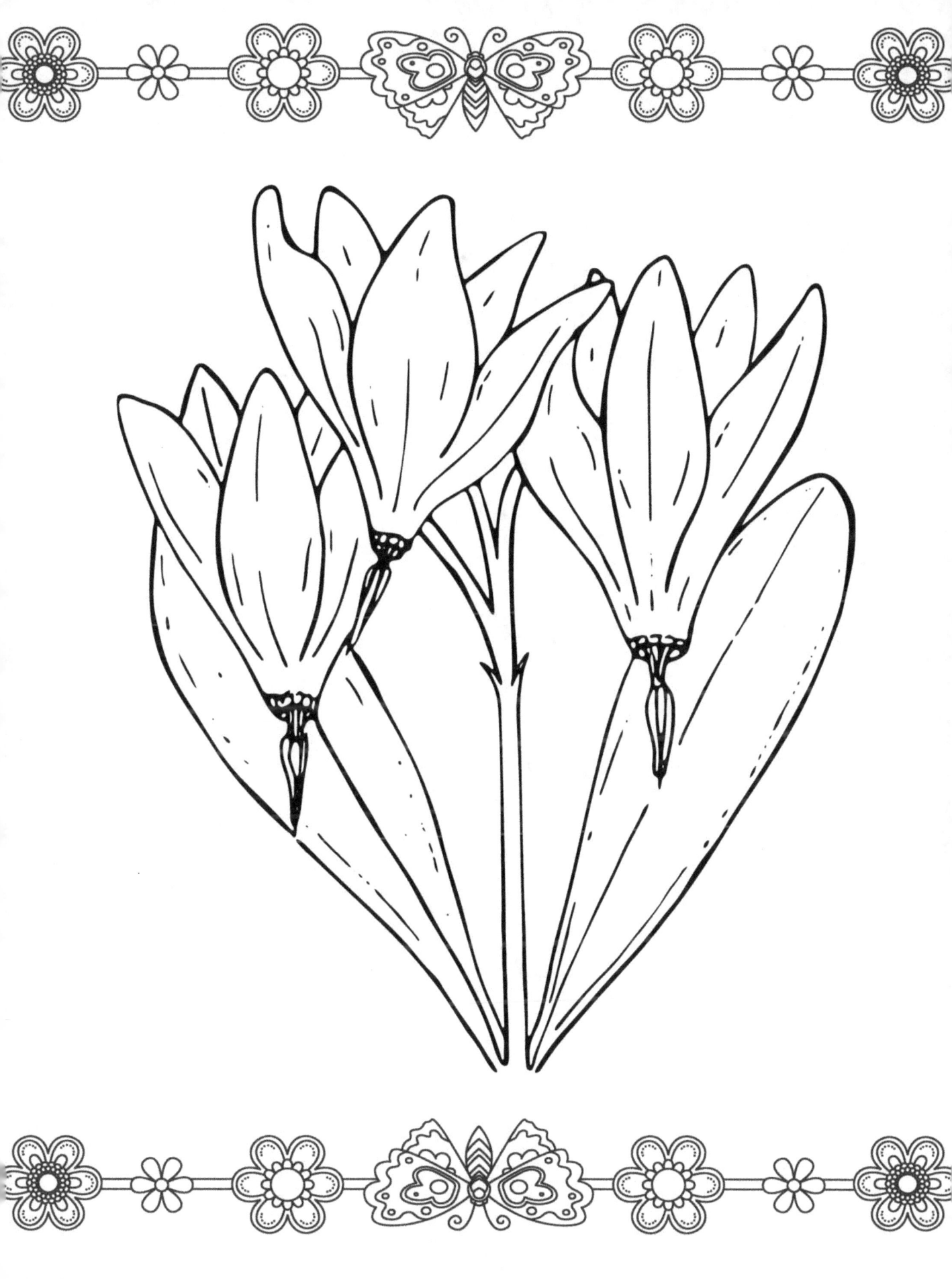

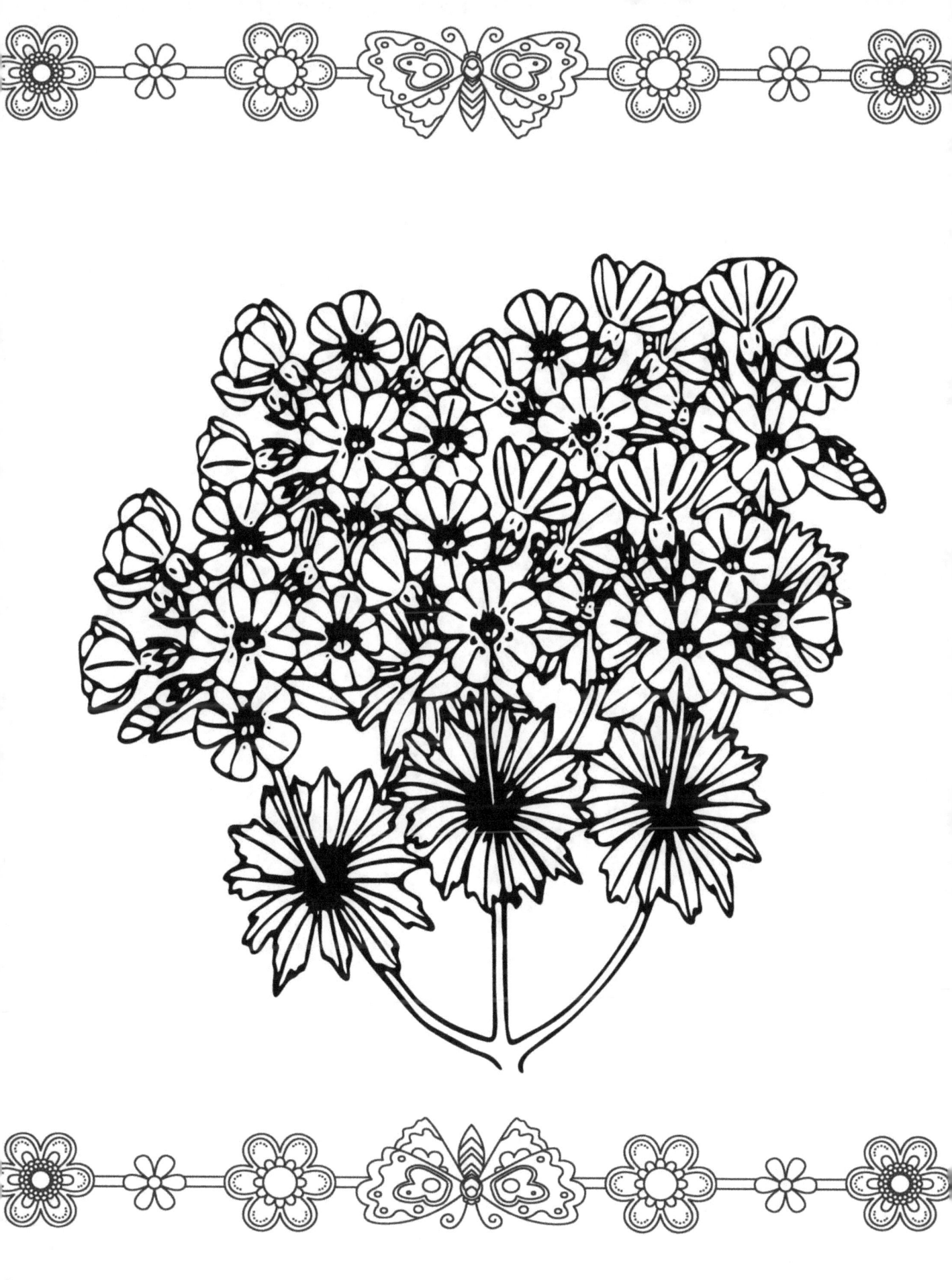

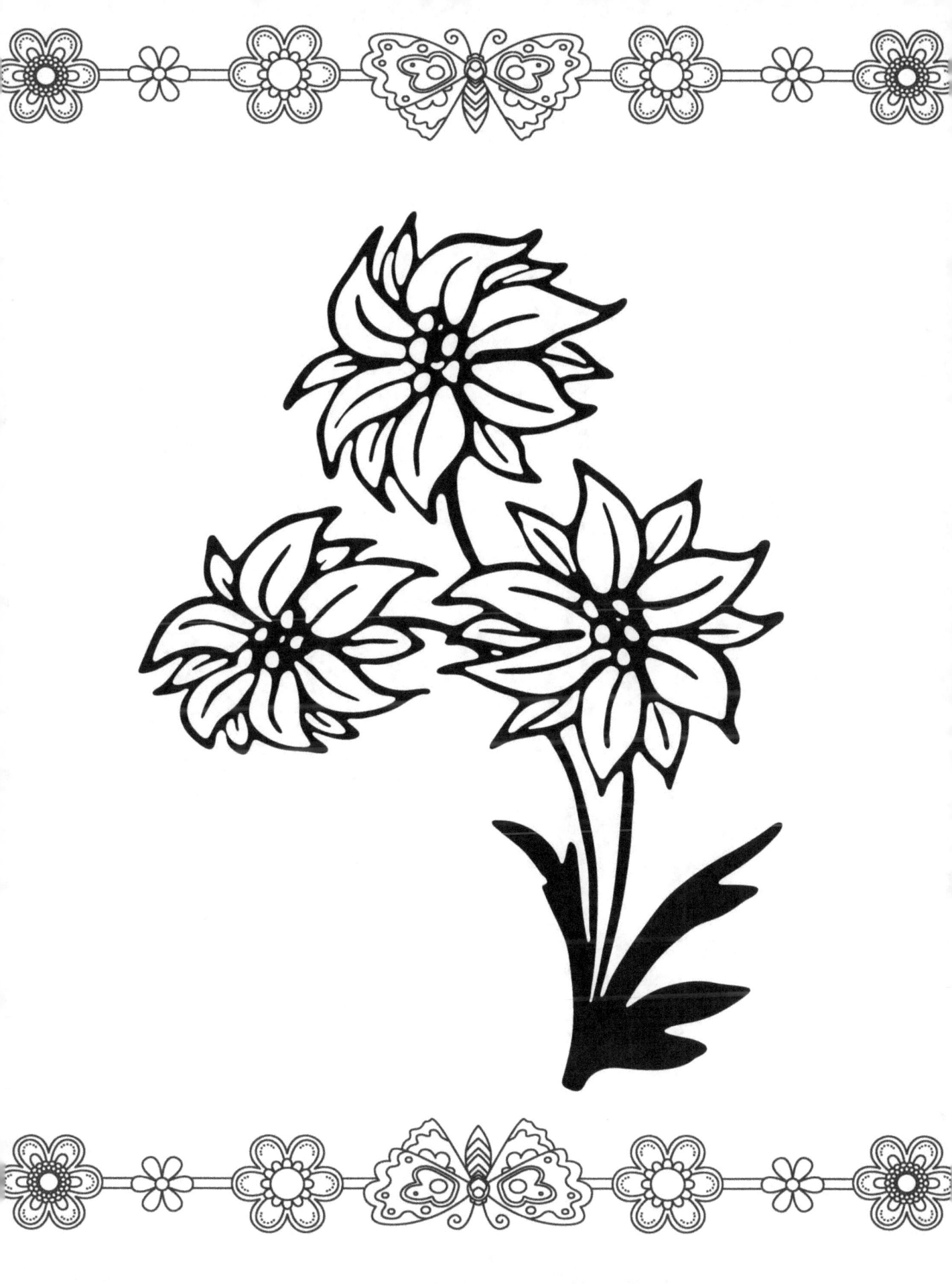

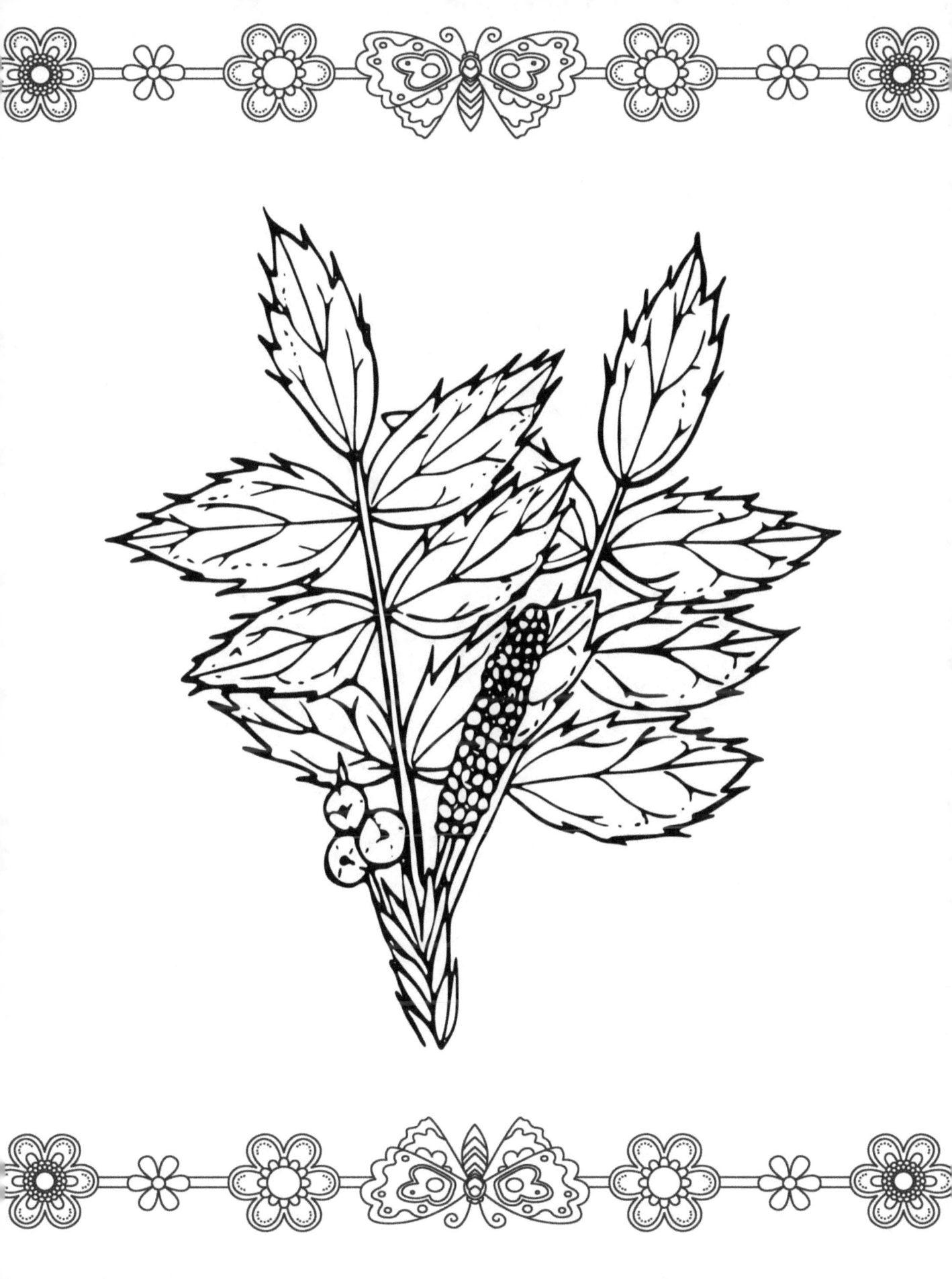

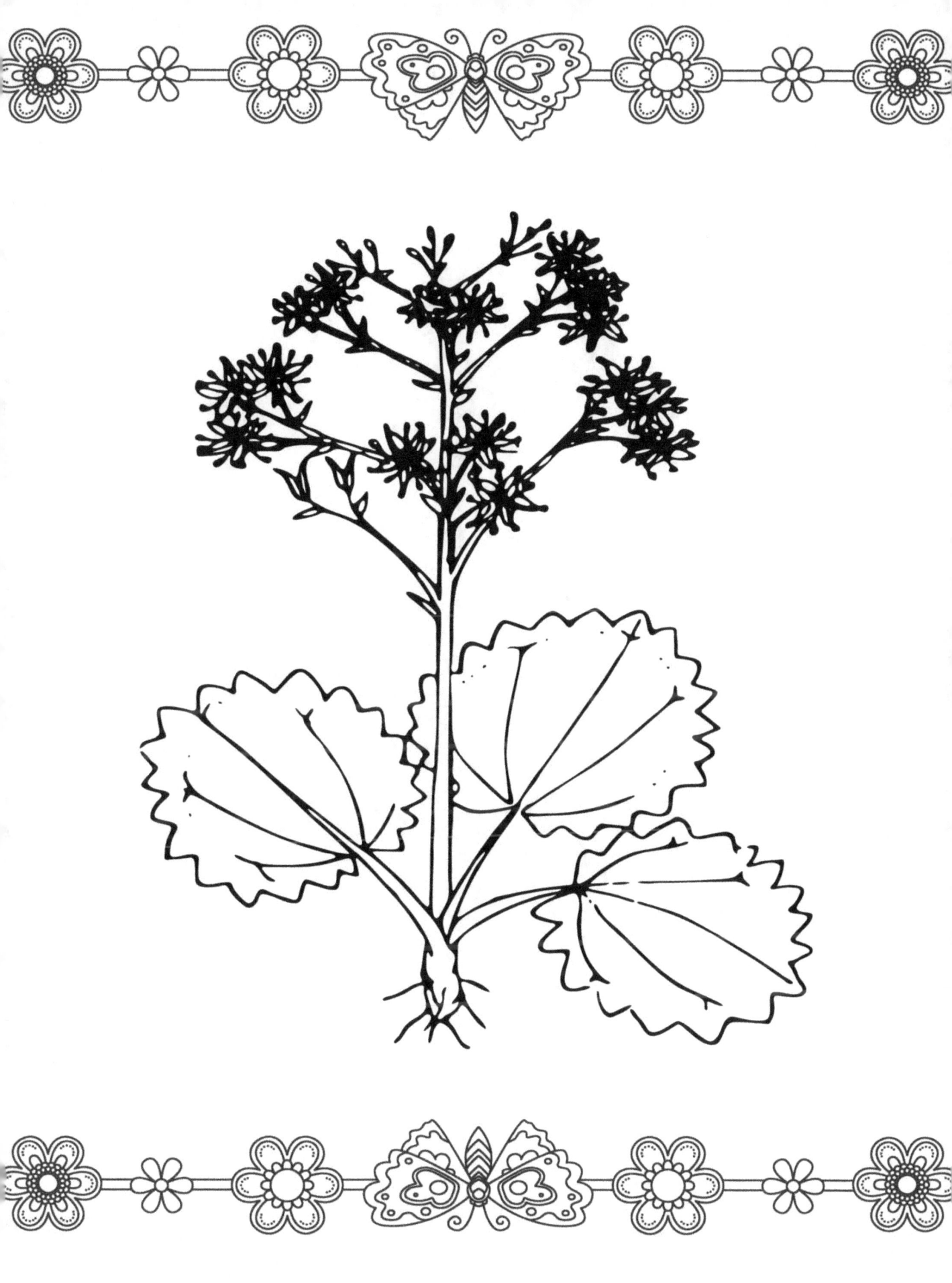

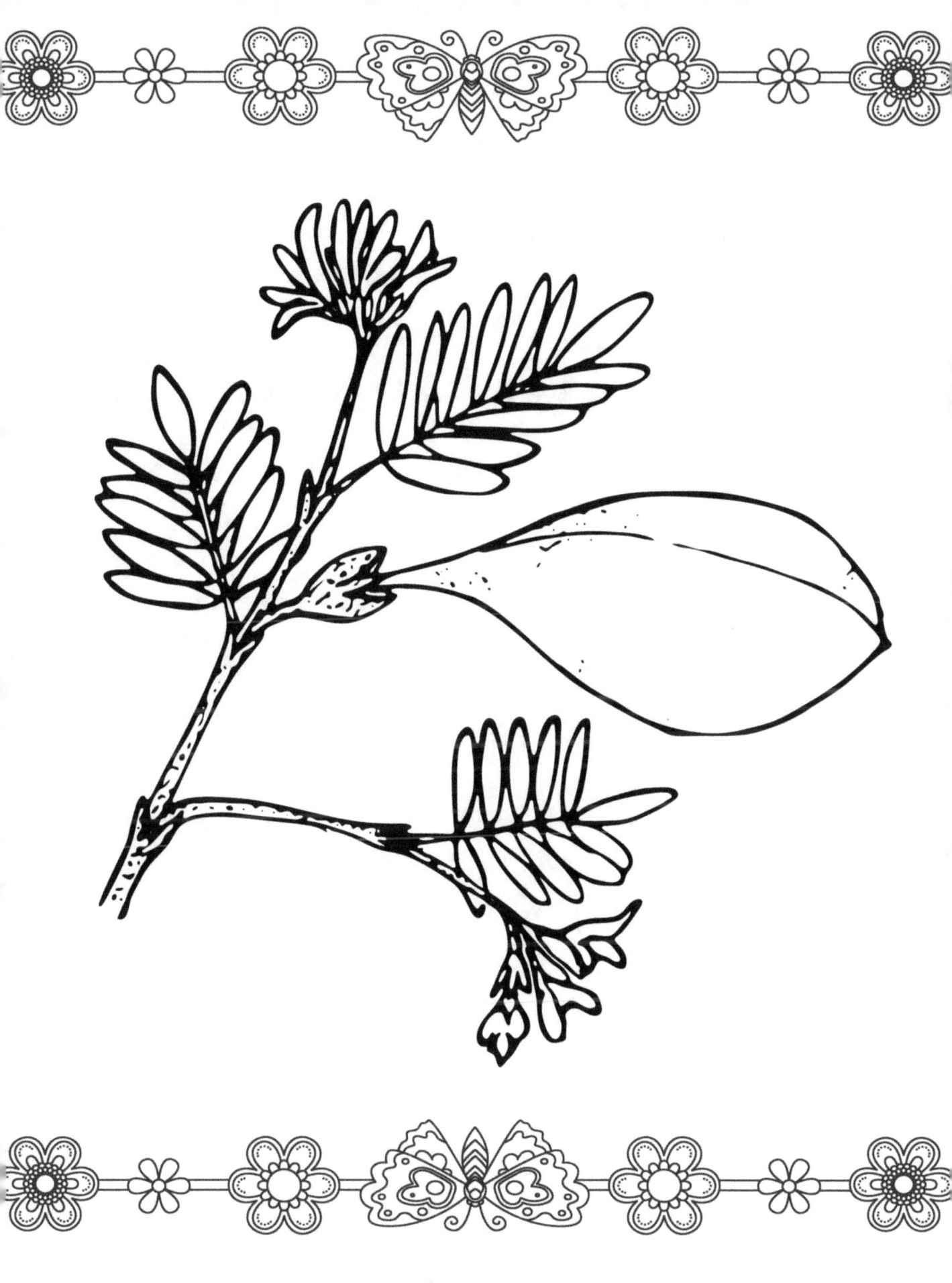

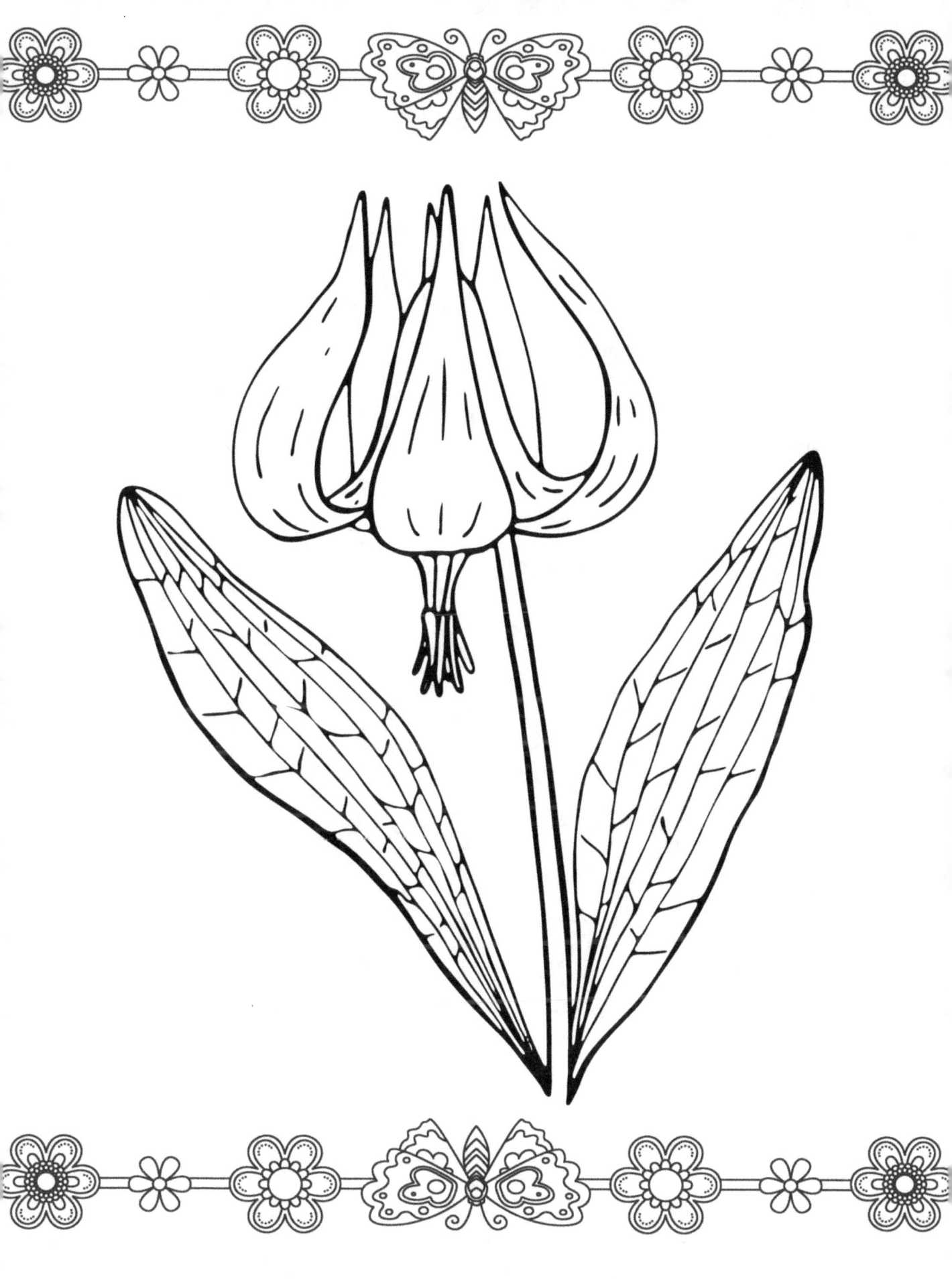

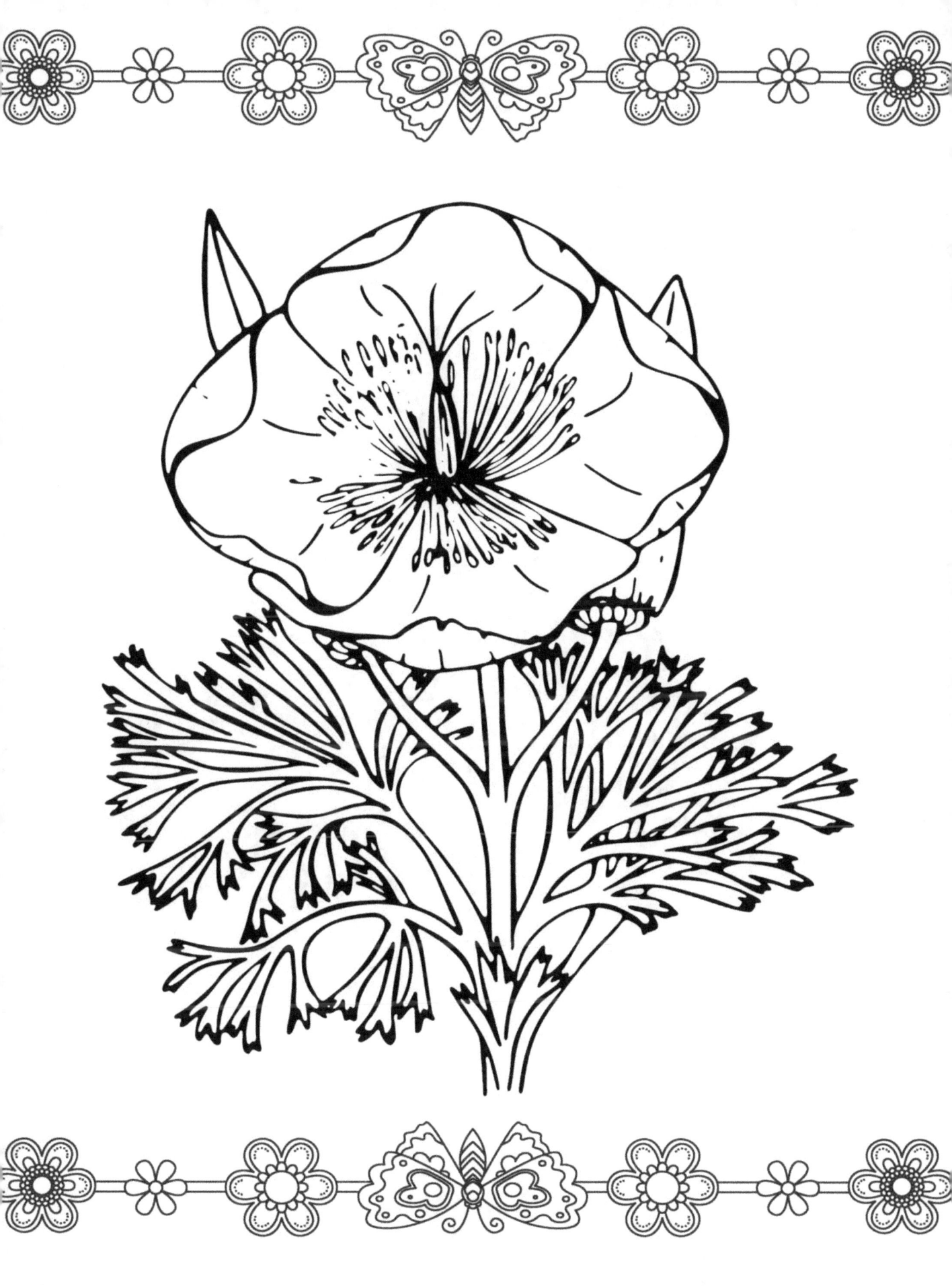

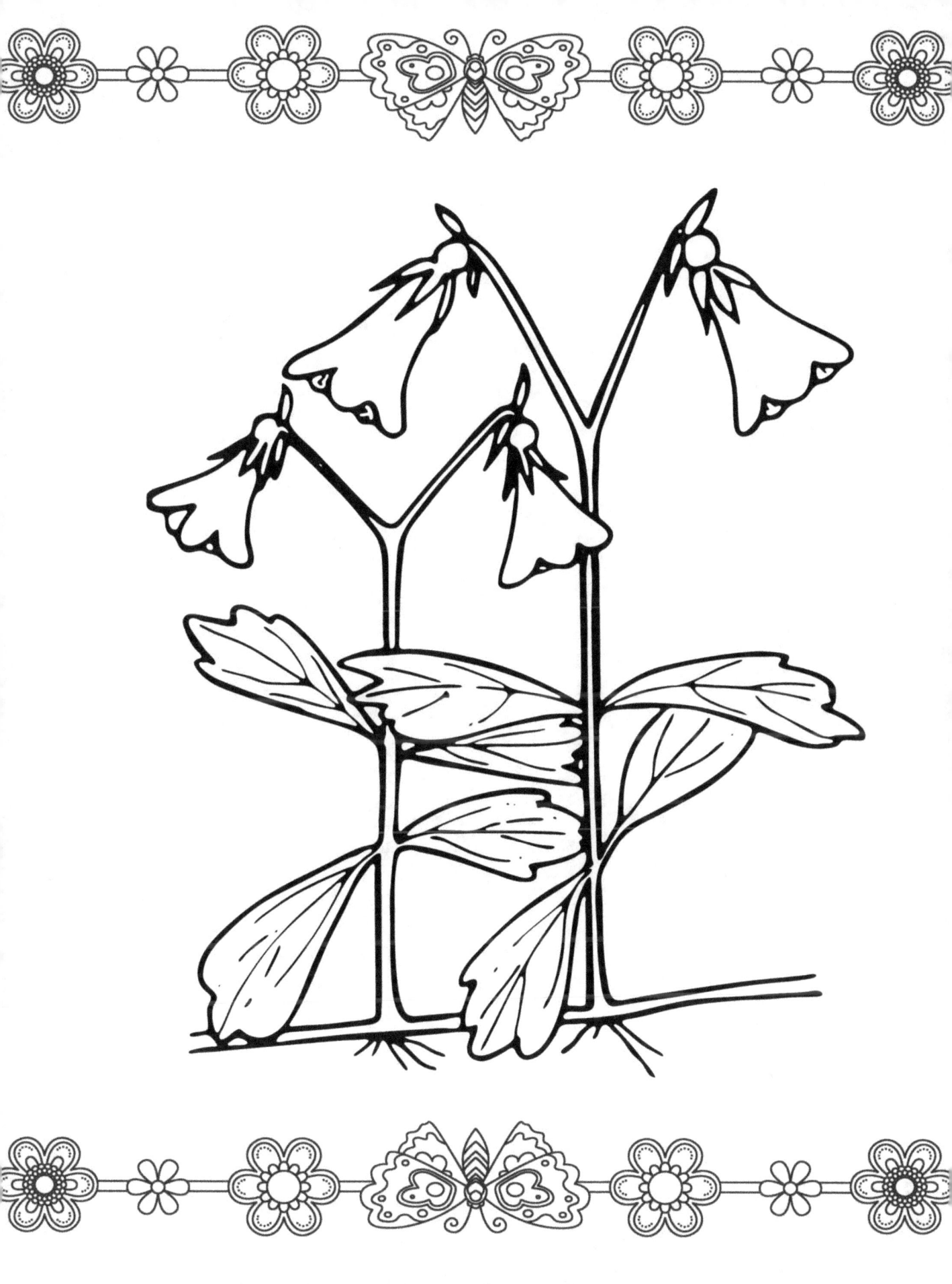

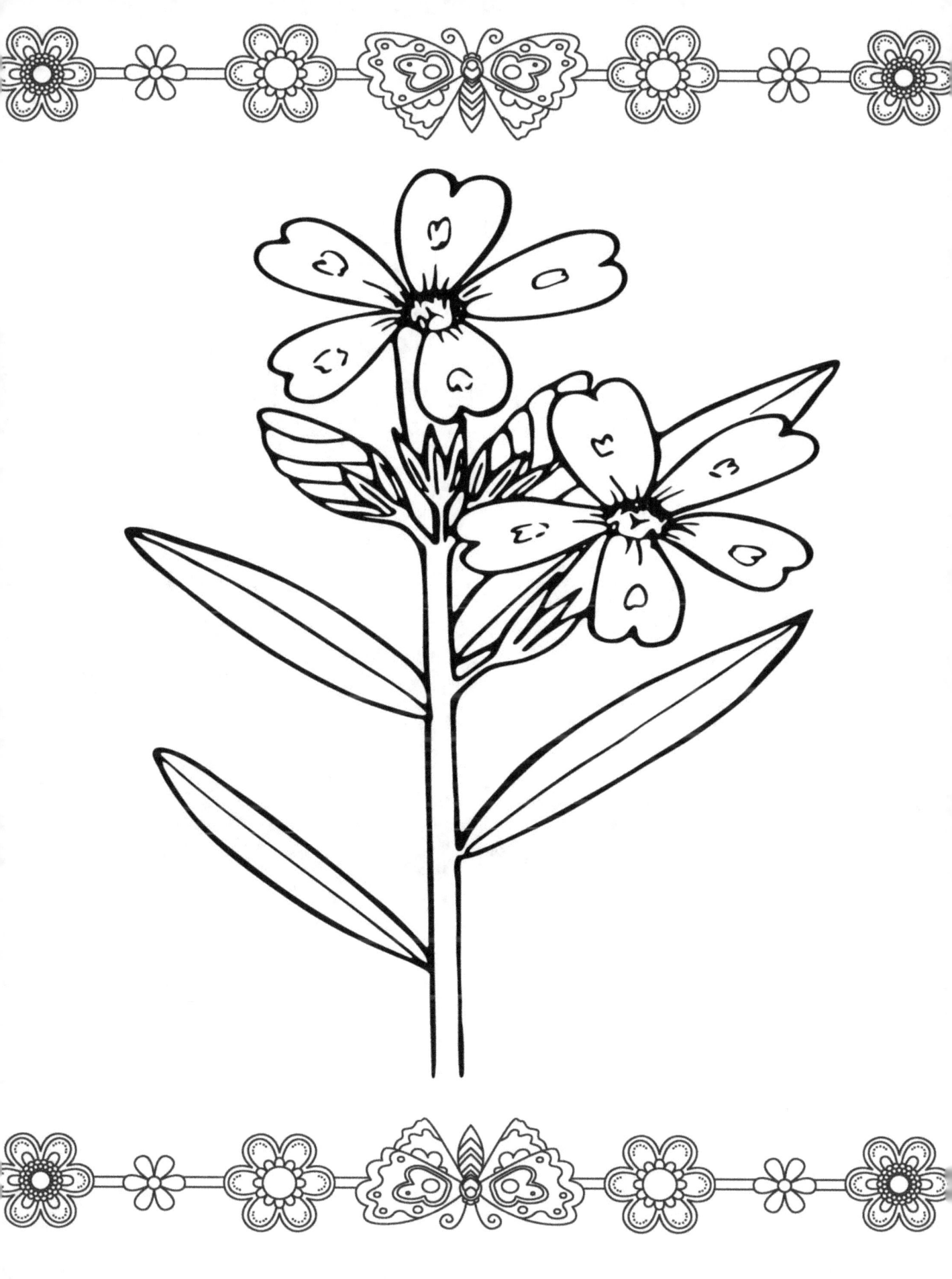

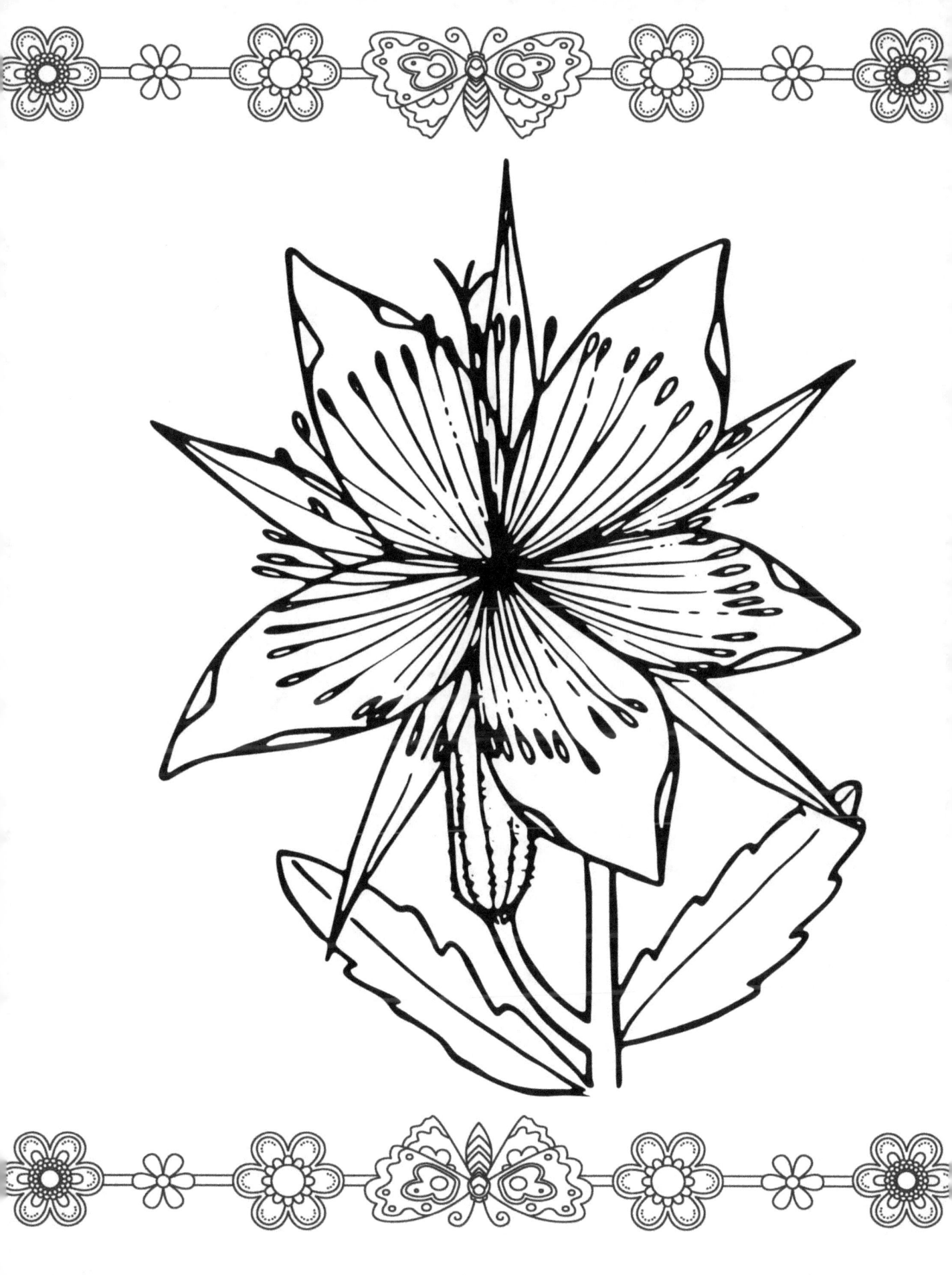

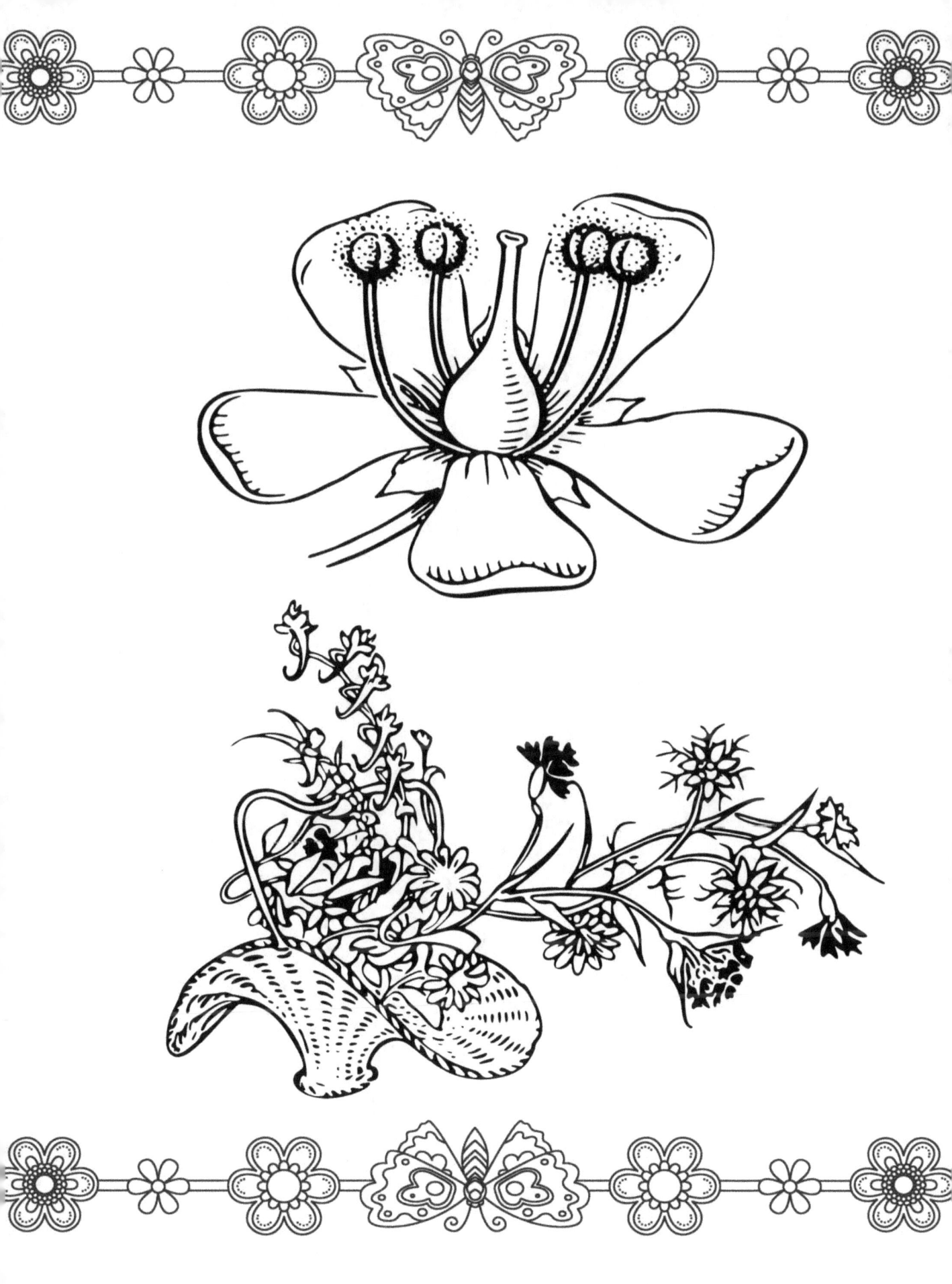

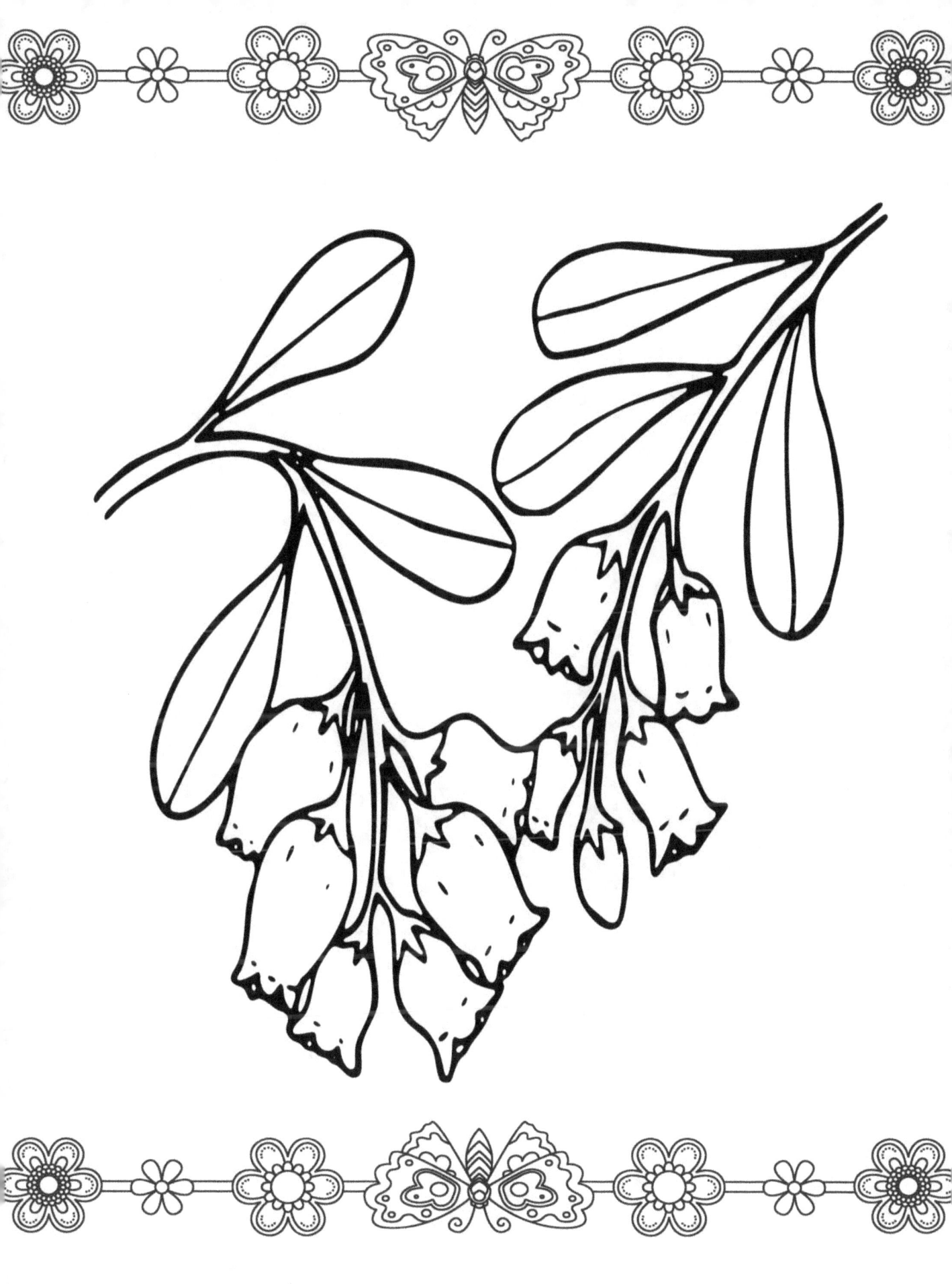

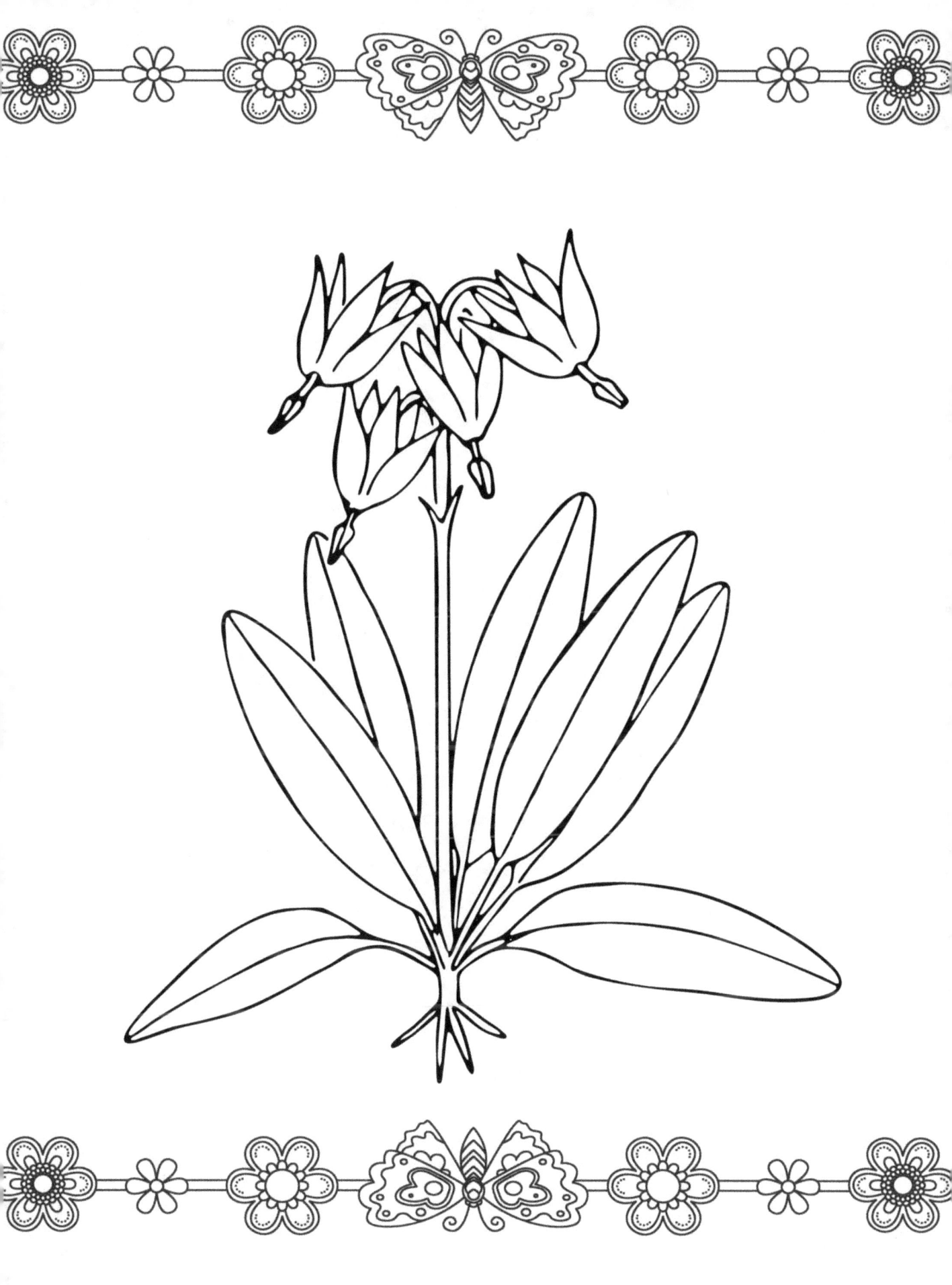

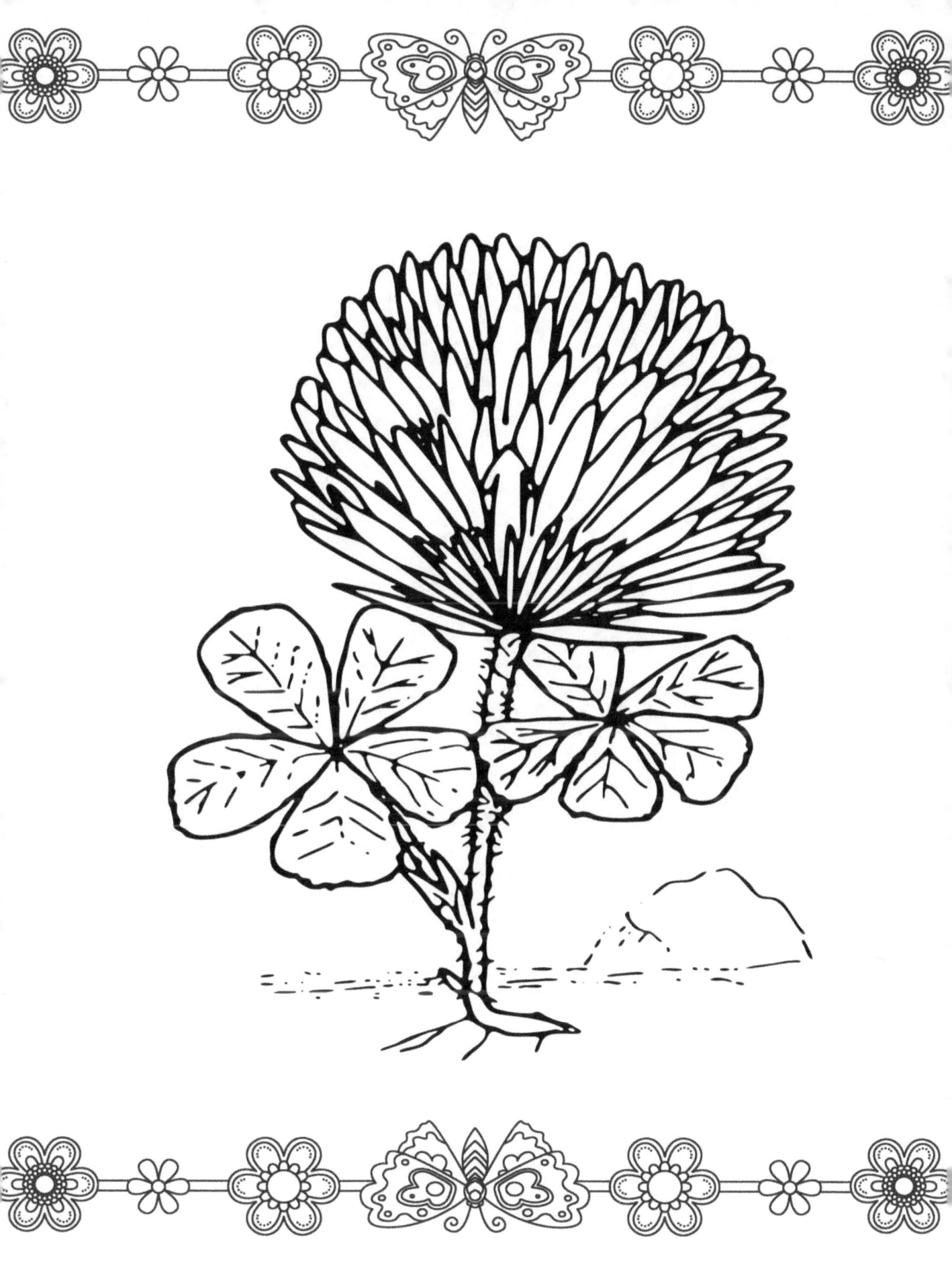

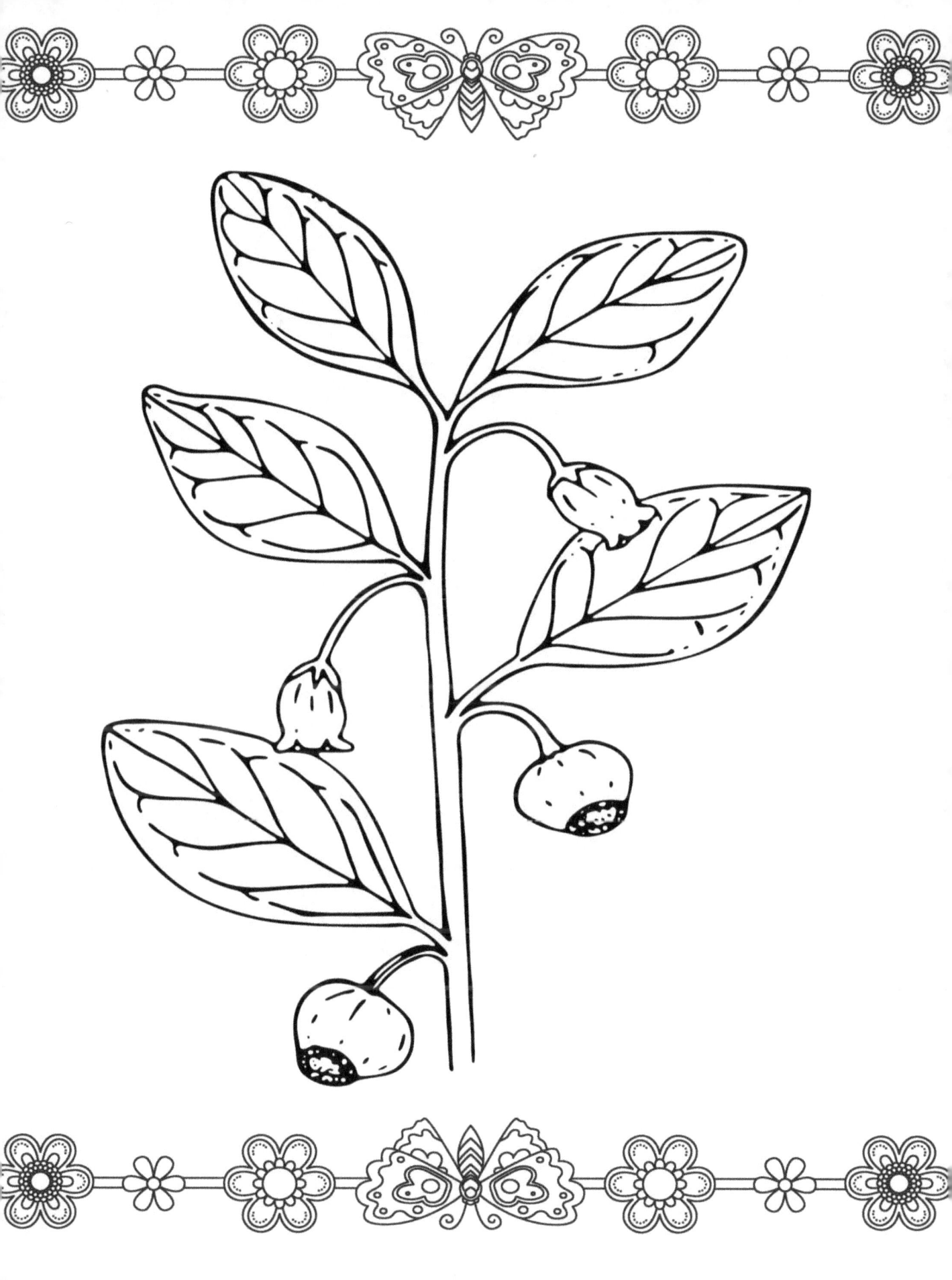

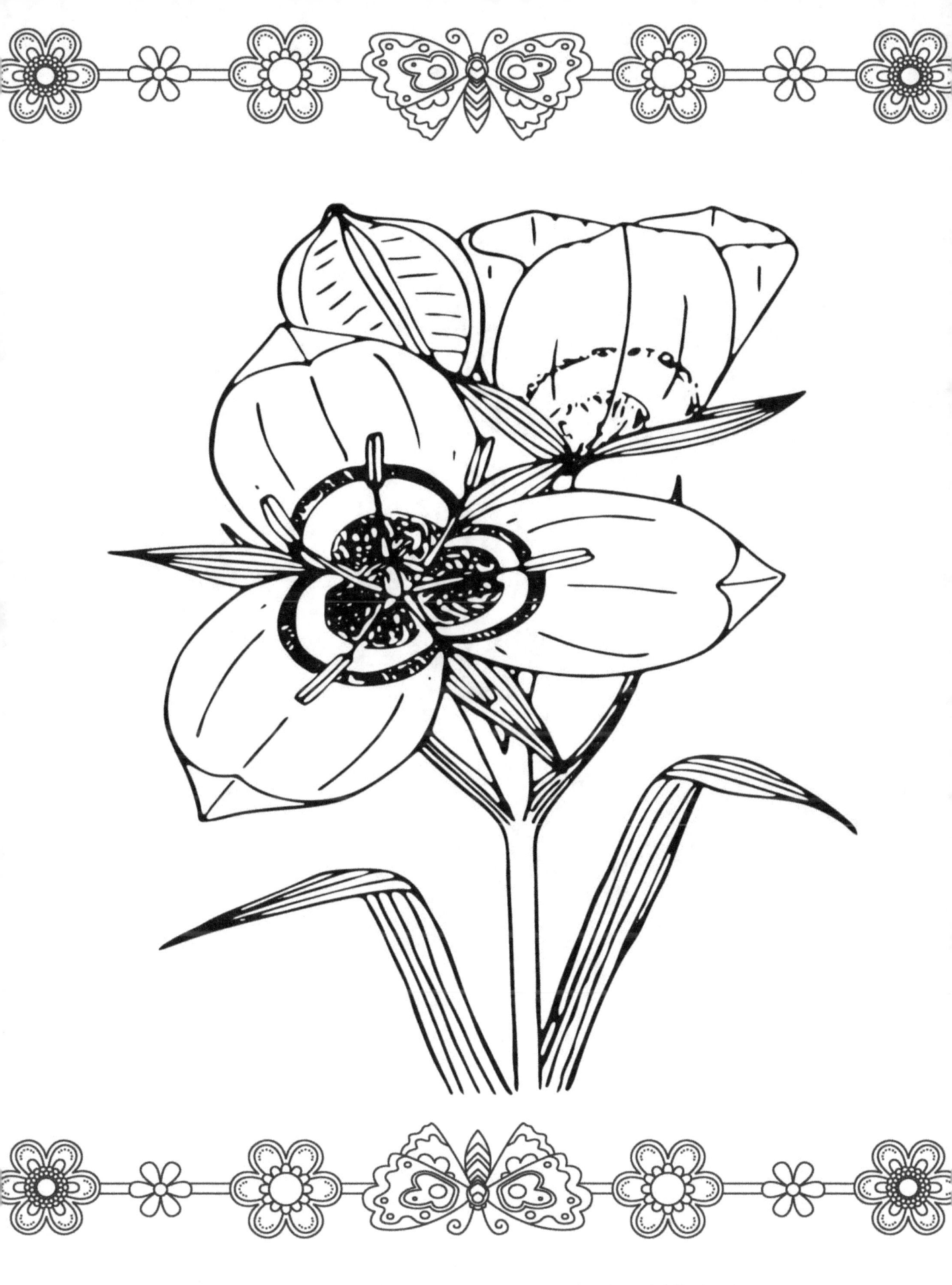

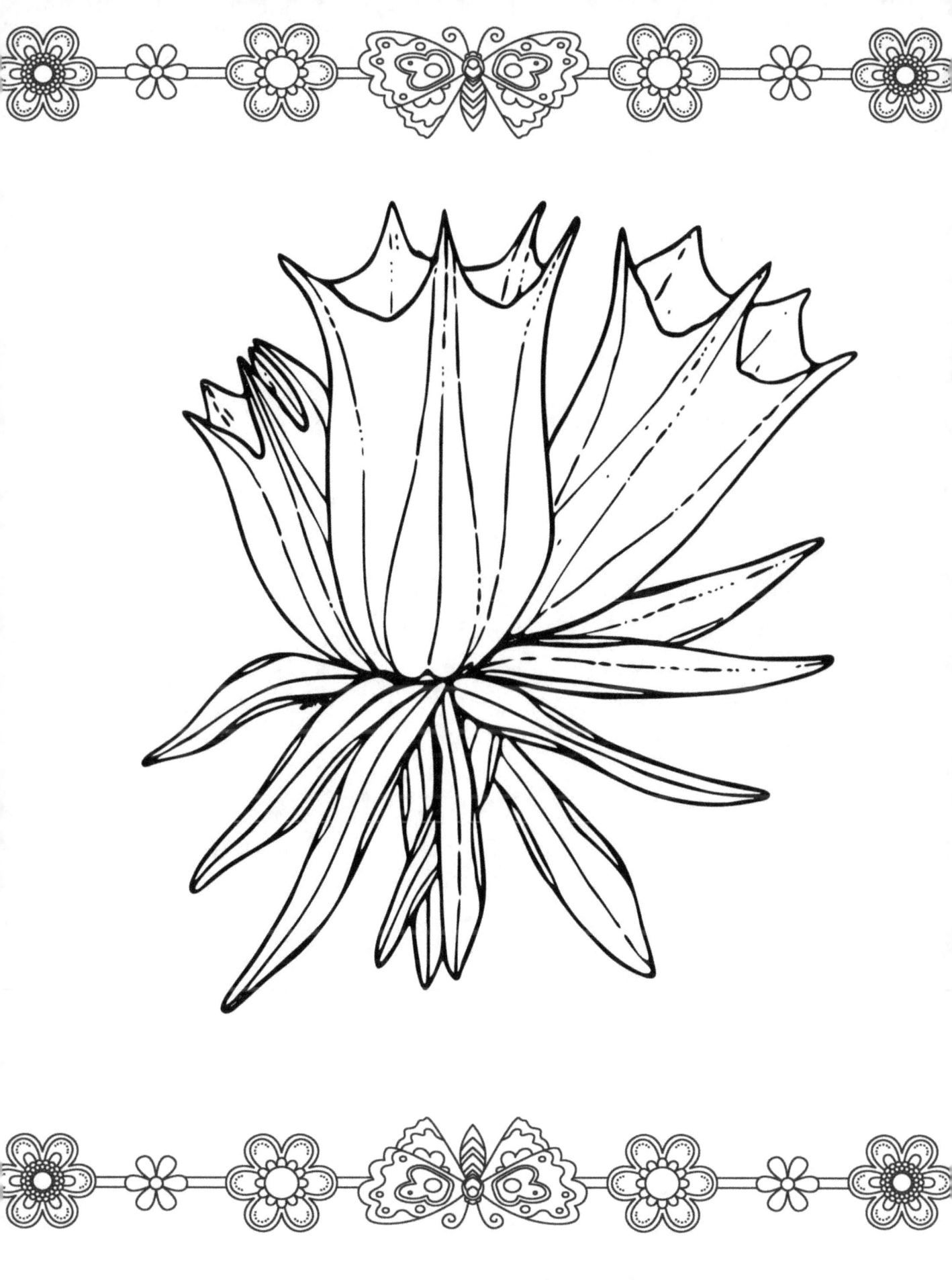

One Last Thing

I hope you have enjoyed colouring the unusual flowers in this book and that you would be kind enough to consider giving an honest review on Amazon.

Also, look out for the other adult colouring books featuring Mandalas and Patterns. There are also some bigger patterns for Seniors or children, all available on Amazon.

See next page for some of my current range

Best Wishes
Charlotte